Counselling People
with
Diabetes

Richard Shillitoe

Communication and Counselling in Health Care
Series editor: Hilton Davis

Counselling People
with
Diabetes

Dr Richard Shillitoe

Consultant Clinical Psychologist, Airedale NHS Trust

Medical advisor: Professor Harry Keen
*Professor Emeritus of Human Metabolism, Guy's Hospital, London,
and Honorary Consultant Physician Emeritus, and Chair of the
Executive Council of the British Diabetic Association*

BPS
BOOKS Published by the British Psychological Society

First published in 1994 by BPS Books (The British Psychological Society),
St Andrews House, 48 Princess Road East, Leicester LE1 7DR.

Distributed exclusively in North America by Paul H. Brookes Publishing Co., Inc.,
P.O. Box 10624, Baltimore, Maryland 21285, U.S.A.

A catalogue record for this book is available from the British Library.

ISBN 1 85433 136 1 paperback

Phototypeset by Gem Graphics, Trenance, Mawgan Porth, Cornwall
Printed in Great Britain by BPC Wheatons Ltd, Exeter

OTHER TITLES IN THE SERIES
Counselling Parents of Children with Chronic Illness or Disability
by Hilton Davis
Counselling for Heart Disease by Paul Bennett
Counselling in Obstetrics and Gynaecology by Myra Hunter

DEDICATION

To Denise and Michael. Again.

ACKNOWLEDGEMENT

I should like to thank Hilton Davis for his detailed and valuable comments at different stages during the writing of this book.

CONTENTS

Preface to the Series

People who suffer chronic disease or disability are confronted by problems that are as much psychological as physical, and involve all members of their family and the wider social network. Psychosocial adaptation is important in its own right, in terms of making necessary changes in life style, altering aspirations or coping with an uncertain future. However, it may also influence the effectiveness of the diagnostic and treatment processes, and hence eventual outcomes.

As a consequence, health care, whether preventive or treatment-oriented, must encompass the psychosocial aspects of illness as well as the physical, at all phases of the life cycle and at all stages of disease. The basis of this is skilled communication and supportive counselling by all involved in providing services, professionally or voluntarily. Everyone, from the student to the experienced practitioner, can benefit from appropriate training in this area, where the social skills required are complex and uncertain.

Although there is a sizeable research literature related to counselling and communication in the area of health care, specialist texts for training purposes are scarce. The current series was, therefore, conceived as a practical resource for all who work in health services. Each book is concerned with a specific area of health care. The authors have been asked to provide detailed information, from the patient's perspective, about the problems (physical, psychological and social) faced by patients and their families. Each book examines the role of counselling and communication in the process of helping people to come to terms and deal with these problems, and presents usable frameworks as a guide to the helping process. Detailed and practical descriptions of the major qualities, abilities and skills that are required to provide the most effective help for patients are included.

The intention is to stimulate professional and voluntary helpers alike to explore their efforts at supportive communication. It is hoped that by so doing, they become sufficiently aware of patient difficulties and the processes of adaptation, and more able to facilitate positive adjustment. The aims of the series will have been met if patients and their families feel someone has listened and if they feel respected in their struggle for health. A central theme is the effort to make people feel better about themselves and able to face the future, no matter how bleak, with dignity.

Hilton Davis
Series editor

Foreword

The title *Counselling People with Diabetes* does less than justice to the broad scope of this book. Its general themes apply well beyond the confines of diabetes and extend to a much more general consideration of the complex relationships in medicine and in society. In a health care scene, which is rapidly changing for both 'patient' and 'professional', it is important to identify and explore those enduring needs and processes upon which humane and effective health care – and disease management – will always be based; and this is the broad outcome of this book.

Diabetes is an excellent working example to describe and define the evolving nature of the roles and relationships of patients, health care professionals and carers. At one extreme there is the old (but still living) medical model of benign authoritarianism. The professional, particularly the doctor, submits the patient to grave consideration then hands down a verdict on what is wrong and what is to be done about it. The doctor is unquestionably and unquestioningly presumed to be actuated only by the purest and best-informed concerns for the patient's interests. In their turn, patients are naturally expected to comply; failure to do so is irresponsible, a matter for regret and perhaps admonition. At the other extreme is the contemporary construct of the therapeutic partnership, in which patients and professionals interact collaboratively to overcome the health problem. These new responsibilities are not always entirely welcomed by the patient, just as the much freer and critical questioning of the methods and even the motives of the health professionals may cause resentment and contention.

The changes in clinical relationships are occurring against the background of major changes in society at large, with increasingly active consumerism of the citizen displacing the more passive and grateful role of the subject. This has also tended to widen the gap in attitudes to health care provision at the primary care level on the one hand and at the specialist level on the other. For many years, communication skills have played a large and important role in the training and work practice of good general practice teams. In many specialist, usually hospital-based, areas, however, while these matters might have received formal recognition, relatively little has been done to introduce them into daily practice. The consultant is still perceived as the king (or queen) of the castle, staffed by a well demarcated hierarchy of supporters and retainers. This structure has been rudely eroded by the management changes and shifts of financial power within the NHS since 1990. Indeed, the new therapeutic partnership may need to influence, if not also include, health-care commissioning, NHS management, trust board chair and chief executives!

The care of the person with diabetes has always been something of an exception to the traditional specialist role and has actually been responsible for a number of pioneering efforts to improve relationships. The general public expectation has driven some of the change, but so has the burgeoning technology of diabetes care. The British Diabetes Association, fundamentally a patient-based organization, has played an important catalytic role in bringing all the parties together in a neutral forum where 'patient power' predominates. The need for self-management and regulation by the insulin-injecting patient has always been evident, and was made explicit by such diabetes pioneers as Lawrence and Joslin in the 1930s. Teaching how to inject, how to regulate food intake, how to monitor first urine, then blood, and how to recognize and deal with hypoglycaemia were always the clear responsibility of the diabetic clinic, sometimes receiving far less than due attention.

The emergence of new methods for self-measurement of blood glucose, new devices for insulin administration and techniques which evaluate success in achieving control (e.g. HbA1c levels) demanded fresh attention to the question of 'patient education' as it was infelicitously called. Inevitably that brought into much sharper relief the concern for patients' attitudes, motivations, perceptions and resistances. The recently published results of the Diabetes Control and Complications Trial (DCCT) represents the clearest possible demonstration of the prime need for the patient to take as much effective responsibility for self-management as possible, as this book brings out. There is now no doubt that improved diabetic control will substantially reduce the risk of the devastating complications of diabetes. It is equally clear that this improved degree of control means a much greater investment of time, effort and commitment all round with the patient taking a leading place in the therapeutic team.

We now clearly know what we need to do; our problem remains how best to do it. It is this challenge which this book takes up. Its broad insights and practical advice are much to be welcomed and, more important, pressed into use.

Professor Harry Keen, MD, FRCP
May 1994

Who is this Book For?

In *The Wind in the Willows*, when the stoats and the weasels had been expelled from Toad Hall, Mr Toad set about organizing a celebration. The programme went like this:

Speech ....by Toad
Address .... by Toad
Song ....by Toad
Other compositions .... by Toad

Evidently, Mr Toad was not a believer in teamwork.

He would not have felt at home in the world of diabetes, where teamwork and collaboration are essential. One of the few generalizations that can be made with any confidence about patients with diabetes, especially about those diagnosed during childhood or early adult life, is that they will meet an awful lot of people during their diabetic career.

For a start, there is the range of medical and nursing staff. Some of these will work from hospital, while others might be community based, depending upon how the local diabetes services are organized. Some will be specialists, such as consultant diabetologists or clinical nurse specialists, with a broad and deep experience of helping people with diabetes. Some will be generalists with less experience and training in the disorder and its effects upon people. Patients will certainly meet dietitians fairly regularly, chiropodists and perhaps a clinical psychologist. These people are usually regarded as making up the core diabetes team, although whether they work as a team or as a looser network of workers with a special interest in diabetes will vary with local circumstances.

Depending upon such factors as age and general health, patients may also meet ophthalmologists for assessment and treatment of the visual problems associated with diabetes; orthotists (shoe fitters) for the design and fitting of appropriate shoes for those with foot problems; and vascular surgeons, neurologists, nephrologists and cardiologists for the assessment and treatment of other accompanying medical disorders. Add ward-based staff to this extensive list, if admission to hospital is required, add the obstetric team in the event of pregnancy, blood-takers, technicians, receptionists, appointment clerks, other support staff and assorted students and trainees; the landscape looks distinctly crowded.

There is also a circle of non-specialist or non-health workers who need to know something of diabetes and its management. This includes teachers, if the patient is of school age, staff in occupational health departments if the patient is in work, and care staff if the patient is in residential care.

This book is directed to all these people, regardless of where they work or the nature of their specific skills and training. Perhaps too, it will be read with interest by patients themselves and by their families. I have written it in the belief that to be fully effective health workers require much more than expertise in their particular and specific subject matter. It is not enough for a doctor to know all there is to know about metabolism and physiology. It is not enough for a dietitian to understand perfectly the principles of nutrition, or for a chiropodist to excel in the care of feet. Helpers must also be skilled in psychological care. Although you cannot cure people of their diabetes, you can help them control it. You can comfort and support those who are in distress because of it. You can explain about the disease to patients and teach them the skills to manage it successfully. These tasks require the use of counselling and other psychological skills. You must know how to build a relationship with patients. You must have an understanding of how patients and families cope and adapt to the changing demands of the disease and treatment. You must learn how to facilitate changes in people, sometimes in their behaviour and sometimes in the way they feel about themselves and about diabetes.

The purpose of this book is to help the reader understand something of these processes, to know when these skills are required and to go some way in acquiring them. This may seem a tall order. If it is largely new ground for you, you may feel de-skilled and bewildered; rather like newly diagnosed patients might feel in the face of all the new events that confront them. However, the book is planned to take you through the tasks in a step-by-step manner in order to make them less daunting and more achievable.

Language and Labels

Given the wide range of personnel involved in diabetes care, the question arises of what terminology to use when referring to them: clinicians; health care workers; health care professionals; providers;

practitioners. The possibilities seem endless. I have chosen to use the general term 'helper' when not referring to a specific occupational group. A helper, after all, is what we are all trying to be, in the context of our own particular circumstances and our own particular professional skills. Although the book is about counselling in diabetes care, I have avoided using the word 'counsellor'. I have done so because the term is often used to refer to someone with a detailed training in a specific school of psychological therapy. When I write of counselling in this book, I shall be referring to the use of counselling skills that are relevant to all helpers, irrespective of professional background or qualifications, and that do not require lengthy specialized training.

When writing about the recipients of helpers' activities, I shall use the term 'patients'. It is difficult to think of a word that adequately captures the state (or status) of a person with a chronic disease in relation to those who are trying to provide some form of professional assistance. The words most frequently used – 'patient', 'client' and, increasingly, 'customer' or 'user' – all have overtones that some readers will find undesirable. 'Customer' implies consumer power, but also market forces; a highly sensitive issue in health services at the time of writing. 'Client' finds favour with many, yet still seems to retain an element of dependency and patronage. The problems associated with the use of 'patient' are well known. On balance, however, I have decided to use 'patient'. One of its meanings is to respond to adversity with composure, and this strikes me as being appropriate for someone struggling with a chronic disease.

Finally, I shall not call someone with diabetes a diabetic. The use of 'diabetic' is usually defended as being a verbal or written shorthand that is not intended to be disrespectful or derogatory, but it does perpetuate an attitude of depersonalization in which the disease, not the person, is the focus of treatment. In addition, many people with diabetes dislike being called 'a diabetic'. For these reasons, then, I shall write about *people* (or patients) *with diabetes* and not about diabetics.

Counselling as a Way of Helping

No single helping strategy is sufficient to meet all the diverse needs and situations that confront the person with diabetes. The helper requires a range of skills and strategies. Hopson (1982) has identified six general types of helping strategy in health care. They are all applicable to diabetes care. There are times when each technique is appropriate and times when each is quite inappropriate. Each forms a part of the helper's complete tool-kit. It is one of the helper's skills to know which technique is best for a particular patient on a specific occasion. The order in which they appear in the following list does not indicate their relative importance.

Giving advice. This involves offering a patient your opinion of what would be their best course of action, based on your assessment of their situation. An example of this is when a doctor recommends to patients who are badly controlled by oral hypoglycaemic medication that they should change to insulin injections.

Giving information. This involves giving the patient the information that is necessary in a particular situation. An example of this is when a dietitian gives a patient information about the carbohydrate content of their favourite foods.

Taking direct action. This involves doing something for someone, or acting on their behalf. An example of this is when a parent gives a glucagon injection to a child in a hypoglycaemic coma.

Teaching. This means helping someone to acquire knowledge and skills. An example of this is when a chiropodist demonstrates to an elderly patient how to take good care of their feet and toenails.

Changing systems. This means working to influence and improve systems that are causing difficulty for people. Multidisciplinary health care teams and families can both be thought of as systems. Examples here include a psychologist focusing on the part played by family interactions in a youngster's adaptation to diabetes, or a clinical nurse specialist introducing a new method of care into a clinic.

Counselling. This involves helping someone to explore a problem and to clarify conflicting issues so that they can decide for themselves what to do. In other words, this involves helping people to help themselves. An example of this is to support a family following the diagnosis of diabetes in one of its members, or to help a young woman with diabetes and her partner exploring their fears and concerns about starting a family.

Listing these strategies in this way gives the impression that they are different and distinct, but this is not so. There are similarities between the strategies and a degree of overlap between them. They all rely on the helper's skills of listening to patients and of making relationships with them. Although it is possible to do things to patients without the need for interpersonal skills (such as giving a glucagon injection to an unconscious patient, or sending a self-help booklet through the post), in normal circumstances the effectiveness of the strategies will be improved when the helper-patient relationship and communication are both good. When teaching, giving advice or information, or when using any of the other helping strategies, the accomplished helper will be using the skills of good communication and counselling.

Counselling requires certain values from the helper, along with specific skills. The main values are a belief in the worth of each person and that everybody has the right to personal autonomy and self-direction. The main skills are listening properly, conveying warmth and interest, asking open questions, and being familiar with techniques that can be used to help patients clarify their goals, and design plans to reach them.

One point to clear up concerns the belief that counselling skills are only relevant when a patient is going through a period of crisis. We tend to think of a counsellor as someone to turn to at times of acute distress, following a bereavement, divorce, or some other trauma. This is an important function of counselling, with many obvious applications in the sphere of diabetes care, but it is only one part of the purpose that can be served by the use of counselling techniques. There is also great scope for what is sometimes known as developmental counselling. If we can help people to anticipate the problems that lie ahead, to identify the signs that warn of troubles or stresses, and enable them to acquire the skills of coping, we will have helped them to become more competent, more confident and more independent. There will be many situations where this aspect of counselling will find a place in diabetes care. Rather than being something special and mysterious, therefore, the skills of counselling are of central importance to every aspect of diabetes care and are accessible to all helpers. The following story tries to make this clear.

Whole-Person Care

Perhaps you have read one of those science-fiction novels in which an alternative universe exists alongside the real one. Although the two universes are similar, they are not quite identical and the differences between them are very illuminating. Half-way through the tale, a gap appears in the fabric of space and time, allowing a glimpse into the parallel universe. Wonders are revealed; a moral is drawn. No such novel has been set, so far as I am aware, in a diabetes clinic, but the potential is undoubtedly there:

On planet Mellitus, Dr Mody is holding a clinic. (If you prefer, you can think of him or her as nurse Mody, or chiropodist Mody, or as a member of any other relevant profession and adjust the details accordingly.) He is waiting for Mrs. Sucrose to appear. She is a rather obese 56-year-old woman who developed diabetes some years ago. Her case-notes record a gradual increase in weight. Her blood glucose results are predictably, if unspectacularly, high. Dr Mody has warned her of the effects of long-term poor control, but to no avail. He expects that the session they are about to have will have the same gruesome inevitability about it as all the previous ones. He will suggest that she make greater efforts to reduce her blood glucose. He will also give her the usual advice about trying to lose weight, hand her a new diet sheet, suggest she take more exercise, and send for her again in six months' time. Both know that the diet sheet will go straight into a drawer and the bathroom scales will continue to gather dust. Both will feel frustrated and dissatisfied.

However, thanks to a temporary suspension of the laws of physics, when Mrs Sucrose hears her name called, she accidentally walks through a hole in space and finds herself in the clinic of the Dr Mody who works in the universe next door. This Dr Mody is friendly and interested and asks about her family circumstances. He discovers that she lives with her disabled husband. He spends some time allowing her to discuss her feelings about this. This leads to an exploration of the difficulties of keeping to a diet when food is one of her husband's few remaining pleasures and they like to eat together. Encouraged by this new interest, Mrs Sucrose feels confident enough to mention some of her worries about diabetes, which she has never been able to do before. She has been scared stiff that she will develop heart disease or circulatory problems ever since a doctor once made it seem inevitable. Since then, she has more or less stopped trying to look after herself properly. This doctor, however, listens to her worries and explains about the benefits of good control and how she might achieve it. They agree that it would be helpful for Mrs Sucrose to see the dietitian. Dr Mody knows that the dietitian will take into account the dietary preferences of both Mrs Sucrose and her husband before suggesting some specific changes in their eating habits. They also agree that an early follow-up appointment would be worthwhile, in two months' time.

Mrs Sucrose walks out of the clinic and back into her own universe feeling much more relaxed, positive and determined than she has for a long time.

The moral of this is that wise helpers attend to their patients' psychological universe as much as they do to the physical one. Taken together, technical aspects of care and psychological care make up a powerful combination. Were clinical audit in place on planet Mellitus, the patients of the second Dr Mody would be found to comply better with their treatment, and they would report greater satisfaction with the care they receive.

Back on earth, the same principles apply. Because the disease and the person with the disease cannot be separated from each other, it follows that psychological care and physical care cannot be separated either. By psychological care I mean more than physical care given in a compassionate and sensitive manner, although this is important. There is a whole range of psychological issues that have to be considered alongside the physical ones. Together, physical care and psychological care make up what is sometimes called whole-person care.

When offering whole-person care, the helper has a number of broad objectives. They look like this:

- to concentrate on the person rather than the disease;
- to create a relationship in which patients feel comfortable and safe, and are able, therefore, to explore their thoughts, feelings and behaviours, especially in relation to their diabetes;
- to identify any psychosocial issues that are relevant and that may influence how the patient reacts to the disease and copes with the treatment;
- to help patients find ways of coping effectively with their diabetes;
- to increase patients' feelings of competence and confidence in their ability to manage their diabetes;
- to give patients a set of skills to help them manage their diabetes;
- to help patients evaluate their management skills and to make changes where necessary;
- to reduce patients' feelings of uncertainty and vulnerability concerning the future course of their disease;
- to help patients achieve as much independence as possible from health services;
- to apply these aims to the family or other carers when relevant.

There is a logical sequence underlying the order in which I have listed the objectives; there is an underlying process of care, with a series of steps or stages that help govern and structure the helpers' activities. The structure is flexible and can be modified according to needs and circumstances, but it is valuable to have such a framework. It helps you to place your activities in context. It helps you to plan sessions, and gives you a sense of direction. Speaking personally, I feel more comfortable when I have a framework that guides my actions, and many of you will probably feel the same. Overall, the steps in the helping process are as follows:

Building a relationship. The first stage is to spend some time getting to know each patient as a person. This is done by showing an interest in all aspects of their lives, rather than limiting yourself to technical aspects of care.

Exploring and understanding. You can then move on to gather relevant facts and information. You endeavour to understand the patient's feelings. You explore problems and devote time to uncovering strengths.

Agreeing goals. On the basis of your understanding, you are then in a position to agree some goals to work towards with the patient. These goals might be concerned with technical aspects of care, but might also include many other things such as improving family functioning or self-esteem. For some patients, one goal might be discharge from regular follow-up.

Facilitating change. How are you going to achieve the goals? Together you must work out a strategy. The options might include mobilizing family support, giving some relevant information, teaching a self-care skill, or making changes to the regimen, depending on the nature of the goals.

Evaluating effects. Finally, you need to discuss and assess the effects of the decisions and actions. At follow-up appointments, necessary modifications can be made and you can work towards new goals, gathering any extra information that might be needed.

And so the process is repeated.

Some of you will recognize the influence of the work of Egan (1986) in this framework. The structure of this book broadly follows the outline I have just presented, although I shall also take time to summarize the main features of diabetes and its management, and to describe how people learn to adapt to and live with the disease.

The Importance of Psychological Care

You might argue that the first Dr Mody as I described him earlier is a parody of care, and, because I wanted to make a point, you would be right. I make no secret of supporting the whole-person care approach, and here is why.

The psychological demands of diabetes

The burdens of diabetes last a lifetime. This brings many worries and anxieties. The person, and probably the family too, have to adapt to the demands of the disease and the management regimen. These demands, like life itself, are never static, so that adaptation is a dynamic and changing process. At some times adaptation will be harder to achieve than at others. Great flexibility is required. This requires self-confidence, and, if possible, a supportive family and other people prepared to help.

Many of the problems and crises of management have emotional and psychosocial causes rather than medical ones. Research evidence supports the clinical experience of helpers that there are close links between psychological adjustment and disease control. Almost certainly the relationship works in both directions: the quality of control affects psychological adjustment, and psychological adjustment affects control. The evidence, scientifically speaking, is not cut and dried, but many studies show a correlation between glucose control and such psychological factors as the existence of mood disturbances or the occurrence of stressful life events. Psychological adjustment can affect control through physiological mechanisms or through changes in behaviour. Links have been demonstrated between the carrying out of management tasks and such things as self-esteem, social confidence and family support. Several studies have shown that stress-management programmes can significantly improve control in some patients.

For most of the time diabetes is an invisible disease. In a crowd you cannot tell whether the person standing next to you has diabetes or not. There is no external evidence to excite sympathy, or any of the privileges or concessions that are generally extended to the sick. The struggle to cope is also hidden. Behind the scenes, however, the struggle is continuous as diabetes management requires constant vigilance. Then, and sometimes in the most dramatic way, it becomes all too visible. Many patients work hard to achieve good disease control. The sting in the tail is that the greater the success the patient has at keeping the disease under control, the greater becomes the risk of sudden loss of control – thanks to a hypoglycaemic reaction. This is a particular problem for patients who take insulin. Hypoglycaemia may occur at any time, perhaps without warning, accompanied by changes in self-control, mood, speech and action. The consequences can range from mild embarrassment all the way through to coma and death, according to circumstance and the severity of the reaction.

Dealing with the day-by-day problems is one matter, but there is also the longer time scale to consider. If patients live in dread of hypoglycaemic reactions and with the demands of daily management decisions, they also live in the shadow of developing long-term complications. Everyone who has diabetes soon learns that the disease is a common cause of blindness, kidney failure, blood vessel disease and other degenerative changes. Although we know something of the risk factors for developing complications, we know less about how far good disease control will prevent them. Everyone wants to know 'Will I go blind?', but there is no easy answer to this question; patients have to live with uncertainty. They will need the support of helpers to cope with this.

The psychological demands of treatment

The only way in which good physical control can be achieved is through patients making changes in their behaviour. Potentially, this can involve any aspect of life: from the highly specific, such as the timing of meals and snacks, to the more general, such as career choice and social activities. It can also mean changes in routines that involve the whole family. However, altering behaviour is difficult at the best of times. Since people do not make changes to the way they do things without good reason, patients need to know a great deal about the disease and its management to be able to carry out the necessary actions and make the necessary decisions. Helpers need to know how to communicate such information, and to teach such skills effectively and with sensitivity.

Like much of modern health care, the management of diabetes can seem to be dominated by technology. This is true particularly for patients who require insulin. From the isolation of insulin and its first administration in 1923, the development of better means of delivering the hormone and of purer types of insulin has been the focus of intensive medical research.

This has been accompanied by improved methods of measuring blood glucose. As the techniques and the technology improve, and as the means of obtaining better blood glucose control also improve, the result is a bewildering and increasing variety of regimens and demands that are made upon patients. Not all will be able or willing to cope with such demands, and not all will have the knowledge, skill or confidence to make informed choices. Helpers must know how to enable such choices to be made, or decisions to be reversed, without the patient losing self-respect if they later prove to be inappropriate.

The need for training in psychological care

Being a person with diabetes is not easy, but neither is being a helper charged with delivering some aspect of diabetes care. For instance, you may find it difficult to respond to the emotional content of a patient's problems. You may feel uncomfortable when patients express feelings of frustration, depression, anger, guilt, fear or other powerful and negative emotions. You may understand that such feelings lie behind the neglect of self-care, but be uncertain how to act on that understanding. In a clinic or on a ward, situations like these occur continuously. You may meet an adolescent in rebellious conflict with parents, a disturbed, 'brittle' young woman, or anxious and overprotective parents who are finding it difficult to give their youngster the freedom to develop. You may feel at a loss when faced with such situations, where interpersonal problems are clearly affecting diabetes control. You may also wonder how to facilitate emotional adjustment in someone whose complications are severely limiting their activities: how are you to maintain hope, yet avoid false optimism? You may want to give support and reassurance to an anxious mother-to-be who is having a difficult pregnancy, but your words, when spoken, sound like tired platitudes.

People who work in the field of physical health are trained primarily to take action and to solve practical problems. Emotions and feelings, however, are not things that can be solved. There is no quick fix for the troubles of adolescence or for the fears of blindness. How much easier it is, then, to forget the person behind the disease, to set the blinkers and to concentrate on physical care. How seductive it can be to pore over a set of figures down-loaded from a reflectance meter; to fuss over an infusion pump; to prescribe the latest dietary additive; to dream about implantable glucose sensors.

These can all be very valuable, but they can also be ways of avoiding the human dimension. They allow us to believe that we are practising real, scientific, health care. The culture we live in actively encourages this; it is the stuff of research awards, glory, career advancement and conferences abroad. Scientific medicine saves lives and makes headlines. This causes an imbalance in which the fundamentals of care are under-valued.

We all know that good dietary management is absolutely crucial to the control of all patients with diabetes, but who ever won a Nobel Prize in medicine by writing a recipe book? We know that good psychological care is of paramount importance, but how many times have you heard the insights of psychology scorned for being impractical, irrelevant, or so blindingly obvious that they can be safely ignored?

You might think that there is an ethical issue here. How far is a patient's lifestyle the legitimate concern of health services? Patients who give up smoking, who eat sensibly and who take regular exercise will almost certainly live longer than their coughing, gluttonous and sedentary counterparts. Are these appropriate subjects for health services, or are they a matter of personal choice? Even if you agree that they are areas where helpers should be involved (and for many obese individuals who have developed diabetes in middle life, routine physical management may consist of little more), you may feel that you lack the confidence or the ability to know how to help people to appreciate the self-damaging nature of their lifestyle and to guide and support them in their efforts to change aspects of their behaviour.

Concluding Remarks

In this chapter I have tried to make the case for the importance of psychological care alongside physical care. The two make up what I have called whole-person care. I am recommending that helpers adopt an attitude that seeks to involve patients in discussions about their care wherever possible, and one that respects them as individuals. Helpers are clearly expert in their own field – they know what is best for the disease – but they may not know what is best for the person who has the disease. For their part, patients are expert in their own field – how they want to live their lives – but they may not know what is best for the disease. Helpers and patients need to pool their expertise to determine a treatment programme that suits both the person and the disease. Helpers delivering whole-person care, therefore, have in mind a process of care and use a variety of skills and techniques to help them. They also need to know something of how people react to chronic illness and the psychological processes that influence how they adapt and cope. The plan of this book, therefore, is to take the reader through the stages of the helping process, beginning with the person with the disease and the problems he or she faces.

Summary

❑ A disease cannot be separated from the person with the disease. It follows that helpers must address the psychological as well as the physical aspects of care. Both make up whole-person care.

❑ Treatment programmes should take into account what is best for the disease and what is best for the person with the disease.

❑ The main objectives in providing whole-person care are:
– creating a relationship in which the patient feels comfortable and safe;
– identifying any psychosocial issues which are relevant and which may influence how the patient reacts to the disease and copes with the treatment;
– helping patients to find ways of coping effectively with their diabetes;
– increasing patients' feelings of competence and confidence in their ability to manage their diabetes;
– giving patients a set of skills to help them manage their diabetes;
– working with families and carers where appropriate.

❑ You will need a range of skills to be an effective helper. The ones that you will use most include giving information, teaching, counselling and advising. All require the use of good communication techniques.

❑ The process of helping involves:
– establishing a relationship;
– exploring the problems presented by the patient;
– agreeing goals;
– facilitating change;
– evaluating the effects of decisions and actions.

2

Living with Diabetes: the Disease and its Management

I remember a patient, a university lecturer, once telling me in all seriousness that her job would be so much easier and so much more enjoyable were it not for the students. In a similar vein, no doubt librarians would be happier without people borrowing books, and politicians would govern with wisdom and humility were it not for the electorate. Perhaps diseases would be a lot easier to treat if they occurred in test tubes in the experimental laboratory, and not in human beings. It is easy to feel this way, especially after a long, hard day, but the disease and the person cannot be separated in clinical practice. First, in this chapter, I shall concentrate upon the physical dimension and give some information about diabetes and the main components of the treatment.

Diabetes: the Disease

Diabetes is one of the classic diseases of medicine. Recognizable descriptions of the symptoms can be found in the writings of Greek physicians from the second century A.D. Untreated diabetes is characterized by excessive thirst and urination, and it was this that attracted the attention of the early writers. 'Diabetes' is a Greek word that means siphon – in one end and out the other! Scientific understanding and rational management, however, did not begin until the start of the twentieth century.

We now know that diabetes is a disorder of the regulatory systems responsible for the storage and usage of the chemical energy derived from food. Glucose is the body's main source of energy. The level of glucose in the blood at any one time is determined by the amount entering the blood stream and the amount leaving it. The main factors involved in this balance are food intake and the rate of entry of glucose into tissues and cells. The activity of the liver is also important, as it is responsible for the storage of glucose reserves. Insulin is the hormone primarily responsible for the regulation of blood glucose in the healthy individual. When the body is unable to produce insulin, or is unable to use it, the symptoms of diabetes occur.

When insulin levels are abnormally low, the level of glucose in the blood rises. The body cannot use the glucose, however, because of the absence of insulin. Glucose reserves are mobilized, but they cannot be used either, and simply contribute further to the quantity of glucose in the blood. Hyperglycaemia is the name given to this state of raised blood glucose. The extra glucose in the blood causes changes in the osmotic pressure of the fluid that surrounds the cells and this causes dehydration: water is withdrawn from the cells and excreted, resulting in further dehydration and thirst. This is the mechanism that underlies the classic symptoms of untreated diabetes: frequent urination and great thirst.

Other metabolic disturbances develop. Fatty acids are released from adipose tissue and fat synthesis is reduced. These cause an increase in the levels of ketone bodies. Some of these, such as acetone, are excreted on the breath. This is the source of the characteristic smell of uncontrolled diabetes. Before the availability of insulin treatment, ketoacidosis, coma and death were inescapable.

Types of Diabetes

Diabetes mellitus is, in fact, a collection of clinical syndromes. It has been apparent for many years that there are two main forms of diabetes. Broadly speaking, patients who develop diabetes in childhood or young adulthood have a different form of the disease to those who first develop symptoms in later life. However, the classification is not perfect and many people do not fit neatly into a category.

Two main classificatory systems are in use. One focuses on aetiology. In this system the two main forms are known as Type 1 diabetes and Type 2 diabetes. The other system focuses on pathology; here the forms are known as insulin dependent and non-insulin dependent diabetes. These systems have largely superseded the older division into juvenile onset and maturity onset types. In this book I shall use Type 1 and Type 2, largely because the other labels can be confusing: some patients with 'juvenile onset' diabetes develop it in maturity, and many patients who are not 'insulin-dependent' actually require insulin for satisfactory control of their disease.

Type 1 diabetes mellitus

This roughly corresponds to insulin-dependent diabetes and to the old category of juvenile-onset diabetes mellitus. In this form of diabetes, both sexes are affected equally. The most frequent age at onset is 14 years. The development of a chronic physical disease at this sensitive developmental stage presents the youngster, and the family, with wide-ranging problems of adaptation. Staff need to be familiar with such issues and to know how to handle them with sensitivity.

Presentation is usually acute, with a recent history of thirst, polyuria, tiredness and loss of weight. Twin studies show a concordance rate of about 35 per cent. So, a genetic vulnerability may exist in a given individual, but a specific trigger is also necessary. Possible environmental triggers include viruses, drugs and toxins, but we do not know what they are nor how they operate. Auto-immune mechanisms are also involved, causing the destruction of the insulin-producing cells in the pancreas.

Type 2 diabetes mellitus

Type 2 diabetes mellitus roughly corresponds to non-insulin dependent diabetes and to what used to be called maturity onset diabetes. It is predominantly a disease of ageing, with more than 70 per cent of patients being older than 55 years. It is by far the commoner of the two forms of the disease, with about 70–75 per cent of people with diabetes having the Type 2 disorder. The majority of patients are obese. The onset is generally gradual and the symptoms can be mild. In some cases the disease is asymptomatic and is only picked up at a routine medical examination, or when long-term complications begin to appear. Common symptoms include dryness of the mouth, fatigue, sensory loss and genito-urinary disorders.

Type 2 diabetes is more common in women than in men. Twin studies show a very high concordance rate, approaching 100 per cent, demonstrating a strong genetic component. There is a disturbance of the insulin-producing cells of the pancreas, but there is also tissue resistance to insulin. Many patients (and staff, sometimes) think of Type 2 diabetes as being a mild form. It is not. Degenerative complications are very common and can be very distressing. Approximately 20 per cent of newly diagnosed patients show signs of complications at the time of diagnosis.

Prevalence

Diabetes is a common disease of affluent societies. Taking Type 1 and Type 2 together, it is present in about one to three per cent of the population. Between five to ten per cent of people over 70 years have diabetes. With an increase in screening programmes in primary care, and the increase in the proportion of elderly people in the population, the number of people with known diabetes will certainly rise in the years ahead.

There are economic and ethnic factors at play. Type 2 diabetes is more common in socially disadvantaged groups. Obesity is linked to family income and eating habits, and this may be one reason. The Type 2 disorder is also particularly common in societies with corpulent, physically inactive populations. Studies show that an increase in prevalence occurs as a society abandons its traditional way of life and becomes more and more Westernized. It is even greater among migrant groups who have the full benefits of civilization. Prevalence is particularly high, for example, in British Asians. The cause of this may be a genetic vulnerability that is exposed by a change in lifestyle, especially the exchange of traditional eating patterns to a diet rich in refined sugars. The stress of being a member of a minority or immigrant group may also be partly responsible.

Patients from minority groups often have poor disease control. This has little to do with the disease as such, but is almost entirely due to communication difficulties and the fact that many helpers know little about cultural differences in religion, language, diet, family networks, traditional healing and views on Western medicine. As we will see, all these have a direct bearing on a person's behaviour and reaction to the disease.

Natural History

Diabetes cannot be cured, but modern management offers methods of control. Patients live on, but become prey to a new set of problems: the long-term complications of the disease. One type of complication is micro-vascular, affecting the eyes, kidneys and nerves. Between 35 per cent and 45 per cent of patients with Type 1 diabetes develop overt renal failure, while retinopathy is among the commonest causes of adult blindness in Europe and North America. Neurological symptoms such as pain or loss of sensation are also common. Macrovascular complications include ischaemic heart disease, cerebrovascular disease and peripheral vascular disease. These are black clouds on the horizon for all patients.

For patients with Type 2 diabetes, large blood vessel diseases are the major cause of premature death and disability. Not only are they more common than in the non-diabetic population, they are also more severe. The mortality risk of people with Type 2 diabetes is more than twice that of age- and sex-matched healthy individuals. About 20 per cent of patients show retinopathy within ten years of the diagnosis, and up to ten per cent will have some degree of painful neuropathy. A significant number of patients show complications at the time of diagnosis, indicating that the disease process has lain undetected for a long time.

The personal, social and economic consequences of such complications are high, and their avoidance is one of the main aims of diabetes management. Some people may be genetically vulnerable to complications, but there is also strong evidence that the level of risk is related to long-term hyperglycaemia. As management methods improve, the risk of developing complications should diminish. A multi-centre prospective study in the US, the Diabetes Control and Complications Trial (DCCT Research Group, 1993) concluded that tight blood glucose control significantly delays the onset and slows the progression of retinopathy, nephropathy and neuropathy in patients with Type 1 diabetes. However, this was at the cost of a significant increase in the risk of hypoglycaemia and of increased weight gain. These might expose the patient to a different set of health risks. In other words, although it is possible to prevent or delay complications, it involves patients in a great deal of hard work, which has to be maintained over several years. A challenge for staff is how to translate the results achieved by a group of highly motivated and self-selected volunteers who were very closely monitored and supported, to the management of the great majority of patients with diabetes. The burdens of guilt that those patients who do develop complications or those who are unable to maintain tight control will have to bear may be considerable.

There are still many uncertainties concerning the relationship between disease control and complications. These have a direct bearing on the treatment goals we set with patients. Although we expect them to monitor and control their disease in order to reduce the risk of developing complications, about 25 per cent of patients do not develop complications irrespective of their blood glucose control. We cannot predict who the lucky ones will be. We do not know the degree of blood glucose control that is necessary to reduce the risk of complications significantly, and whether this is the same for all patients. However, although current treatment methods enable patients to improve their glycaemic control, long-term control remains elusive. Even with intensive treatment and support, few patients are able to maintain normal levels of blood glucose over long periods of time.

The Management of Diabetes Mellitus

Medical treatment is initiated to relieve acute symptoms and to reduce the likelihood of long-term problems. From the point of view of the patient, these broad goals have to be translated into a number of self-management tasks, which make up what has been described as the diabetic way of life. The main management tasks are:

- eating a specified diet at appropriate times to attain and maintain appropriate body weight;
- taking medication in the correct dosage at appropriate times to help keep blood glucose as near normal as possible;
- taking exercise and other preventative measures appropriately to improve and maintain good physical condition;
- self-monitoring of blood (or urine) glucose accurately and regularly to obtain feedback about the success of self-management and to direct future efforts.

Management by diet

All patients with diabetes have to regulate their food intake. Children and adolescents need to maintain normal growth and body weight. Adults should try to keep their body weight within the normal range. For those who are obese, weight reduction has many health benefits.

At its simplest, for the non-obese patient with Type 2 diabetes dietary regulation may consist of little more than advice to avoid sugar and sweet things. For the patient who is obese, reduction in energy intake will be necessary if weight loss is to be achieved.

For the patient with Type 1 diabetes and the insulin-treated Type 2 sufferer, matters are more complicated, as attention has also to be paid to the timing of meals as well as their content. This is to prevent swings of blood glucose, because of the limited active time span of injected insulin.

Although the broad principles of dietary management are agreed, nutritionists debate the extent to which added dietary fibre can improve glycaemic control, the optimal nature and amount of dietary fat, the proportion of total energy intake that should derive from carbohydrate, and the role of very low carbohydrate diets. These and other aspects such as the value of 'diabetic' foods and low-sugar beers, cause great confusion in the minds of patients who have seen many dietary recommendations come and go over the years. Furthermore, although modern advice is for a high-carbohydrate, low-fat diet, which represents healthy eating habits for all family members, it does not conform to most people's dietary habits.

The major problem is to change eating habits. To be on a diet need imply neither hunger nor deprivation. However, there is a lot more to food than simply eating when you feel hungry. People eat for many reasons, of which hunger and the need for nutriment are not always the most important. Almost every major personal and social event in a person's life is accompanied by eating. Birth, marriage, parenthood and death are celebrated with special meals. Anniversaries, changing a job, retirement and other significant events also regularly involve eating and drinking. The major events in the calendar of all the world's great religions are marked by periods of either feeding or fasting. Food, therefore, occupies a complex place in society.

Eating is also closely connected to a person's emotional life. Eating patterns are often disturbed during periods of upheaval. People may go off their food when they are upset or worried, or they may comfort eat if they feel lonely and vulnerable. There is a close connection in many families between the giving of food and the giving of affection.

These influences apply to people with diabetes as much as they do to healthy individuals, and they all contribute to the difficulties of changing eating behaviour. The complex functions served by food are seen most clearly when we try to treat patients from other cultures, for whom our dietary advice often fails most profoundly. For example, Asian patients, especially women, live in a culture that encourages family cooking and eating. Dieting or eating a restricted range of foods may represent a threat to the patient's full involvement in their social network. For these reasons, dietary recommendations alone, without a full understanding of the patient in their social and interpersonal network, are often unsuccessful.

Management by insulin

Insulin is required by all patients with Type 1 diabetes from the moment of diagnosis. It is easy to devise an insulin regimen that will remove the primary symptoms of hyperglycaemia; it is much harder to develop a regimen that will result in normal blood glucose over prolonged periods.

In the healthy person, the body's natural pattern of insulin release is a low background output, supplemented by 'spurts' at mealtimes in response to food. To mimic this, a regimen of up to four injections per day is often recommended. This consists of a night-time injection of slow-acting insulin to provide the basal level, and an injection of rapid-acting insulin before each meal. The patient has to adjust the amount of insulin according to current blood glucose, the amount of carbohydrate to be eaten, and predicted activity levels.

Multiple daily injections are used to improve glucose control. They are also valuable for patients who require a more flexible regimen because of their lifestyle. To make demanding regimens more accept-able and more convenient, many patients now use a pen injector; a fully self-contained syringe about the size of a fountain pen that contains a vial of insulin. Patients like pen injectors, but there is no evidence that their usage alone is sufficient to result in improved glucose control. The feeling of greater psychological control that they give the user, however, is very important.

Patients with Type 2 diabetes may require insulin in addition to the main forms of therapy for this type of diabetes (diet, and medica-tion taken orally) for adequate glucose control. Insulin is prescribed for obese patients who cannot lose weight, and for normal-weight patients who are receiving the maximum dose of oral treatment. The avid pursuit of normoglycaemia in patients with Type 2 diabetes, however, is controversial. This is because the frequency of complica-tions, especially cardiovascular disease in patients developing Type 2 diabetes in middle or later life, may be due at least in part to a genetic vulnerability, rather than to long-term hyperglycaemia. Until this question is resolved, clinical practice is to aim at as good glycaemic control as is feasible, with certain common sense exceptions, such as the very old and those whose life expectancy is limited by other medical conditions. The most common insulin regimen for insulin-requiring patients with Type 2 diabetes is a twice-daily injection of a mixture of short- and intermediate-acting insulins, before breakfast and before the evening meal.

Technical advances are not necessarily widely applicable. In continuous subcutaneous insulin infusion (CSII) patients administer insulin not by regular injections but by means of an infusion pump. These pumps are battery powered, worn on a belt and con-stantly deliver a small amount of insulin subcutaneously through an indwelling needle. The patient increases the rate of infusion immediately before each meal to cover the carbohydrate that is about to be eaten. Excellent short-term results can be achieved using CSII, but not all patients can cope with it, probably because the technique requires extra vigilance and close monitoring. Many who start CSII later choose to return to conventional regimens, even though the level of control they achieve may not be so good. Over-optimistic expectations transmitted to patients by their doctors, may have led to the assumption that less personal responsibility for their diabetes control was required than with injections. Some doctors may refer to CSII pumps as though they controlled blood glucose levels, thereby minimizing the part played by the individual actually wearing and using them (Bradley et al., 1987).

Hypoglycaemia

Unfortunately, blood glucose regulation is not a precise science. Many factors influence glycaemic control besides the dose of injected insulin. These include feeding, fasting, exercise, injection site, level of insulin sensitivity and levels of hormones that oppose the action of insulin. These hormones, the stress hormones, are released as part of the stress response, irrespective of whether the stress is psychological or physiological. They are released, for example, when the body's feedback mechanisms detect falling blood glucose. They give rise to symptoms such as sweating, shaking and profound hunger. If the patient can recognize the symptoms for what they are, and not confuse them with anxiety or other forms of psychological stress, corrective action can be taken in the form of extra glucose.

Hypoglycaemia is common and unpleasant. A hypoglycaemic episode – also known as an insulin reaction – can result in physical injury or may be fatal. It is no wonder that hypoglycaemia is a major fear of most insulin-treated patients. This is especially true of episodes in which the normal warning symptoms are missing, and the first signs are those of mental confusion and impaired judgement as the brain becomes starved of energy. The early warning symptoms tend to reduce with the duration of diabetes, and, to the annoyance of the well-controlled patient, with good blood glucose control.

Any regimen designed to produce normal blood glucose also carries a risk of hypoglycaemia. Severe hypoglycaemia, requiring outside assistance for recovery, affects at least 30 per cent of insulin-treated patients at some time in their lives. Intensive insulin regimens increase the frequency of severe episodes by as much as three times over rates seen in conventional regimens. Repeated severe hypoglycaemic episodes can result in the driving licence being withdrawn, perhaps causing financial problems as well as personal inconvenience. Severe insulin reactions can also cause a slight, but measurable, loss of intellectual ability, especially if they occur repeatedly in the very young. A concern of many patients is whether the newer 'human' insulin preparations reduce the warning symptoms of low blood glucose.

The story of human insulin. This is not, as the name implies, insulin of human origin, but animal insulin that has been genetically engineered to resemble human insulin. The way in which it was introduced into clinical practice is a sorry tale of medical paternalism and commercial profiteering.

Despite the assumption that a long process of clinical trials would be necessary to exclude the possibility of adverse effects, the new insulins largely replaced the old ones during the 1980s and without such studies being performed. Many patients whose diabetes was well controlled with animal insulin were transferred to human insulin without medical supervision. This is counter to long-established ethical principles that medication should not be changed simply because newer preparations become available. It clearly occurred for commercial reasons.

Many patients began to complain of reduced warning symptoms of hypoglycaemia. Consequently, clinicians and researchers have been forced to engage in a rearguard action to try to determine how such complaints can be explained. Possibilities include differences in action or structure between the two types of insulin, the insensitivity with which the changeover was made, or the drive to achieve much tighter blood glucose control that occurred at the same time.

There is evidence that the patients who report problems are more likely to have been transferred to human insulin without consultation or discussion. There is also less evidence of such problems occurring in countries where greater flexibility and consultation during the transfer process seem to have been the norm. It is sad to think that while we can engineer insulin successfully, we cannot regulate the process of its introduction into clinical practice. This represents a failure to implement psychological care:

> *'If any good comes from the current unpleasantness it will be to remind everyone that diabetes is an important medical and social problem . . . Diabetes mellitus is a complicated disease that demands close co-operation between the patient and the diabetes care team.'*

(Egger et al., 1992)

Management by oral hypoglycaemic agents

Oral medication is only effective in patients who retain some degree of insulin secretion. It has no place in the treatment of Type 1 diabetes. If diet fails to achieve adequate metabolic control in patients with Type 2 diabetes, a drug from the sulphonylurea group is often prescribed. Although their mode of action is not fully understood, these drugs stimulate insulin secretion, lower blood glucose and improve insulin sensitivity. They are not always effective, however, and they may lose their effectiveness over the years. They carry a significant risk of hypoglycaemia. Tablets from the biguanides group are sometimes used in patients who are obese, usually in conjunction with a sulphonylurea. Such combination therapy is usually undertaken to delay or avoid insulin therapy, when treatment with one oral agent has failed.

Management of lifestyle

The prognosis of diabetes is not purely dependent upon the quality of control of blood glucose, but also on the correction of frequently associated disorders, such as hypertension, obesity and lipid abnormalities. These in their turn are associated to some degree with unhealthy lifestyles, especially smoking, lack of exercise and poor dietary practices. A comprehensive management programme, therefore, also aims to modify these risk factors. This often requires broader-based lifestyle changes, which can be hard to make and harder to maintain.

Exercise. Regular exercise can assist with weight loss and improve insulin sensitivity. It can decrease coronary heart disease risk factors and can give a feeling of well-being. Despite the benefits, exercise can be hazardous unless certain precautions are taken. For patients with Type 1 diabetes, there are risks of hypoglycaemia during and after exercise, when modifications to insulin and carbohydrate intake may be necessary. Patients with Type 2 diabetes treated with sulphonylureas are also at increased risk of exercise-induced hypoglycaemia, although the risk is not so great. For patients with complications, exercise may be harmful, so for all these reasons it is unwise to start an exercise programme without prior medical advice. Once given the go-ahead, there are then the practical questions of how much and how often; how to incorporate exercise into normal lifestyle so that it is more likely to be maintained; and how to avoid the dangers of exercise.

Smoking and drinking. Smoking, with its cardiovascular risks, is a major hazard for people who are already vulnerable to vascular disease thanks to their diabetes. The prevalence of smoking among patients with diabetes, however, is no lower than it is in the non-diabetic population. This is particularly disappointing as many patients are in regular contact with their doctor, nurse specialist or hospital clinic and, almost certainly, will have been informed many times of the dangers of smoking.

Alcohol has effects upon carbohydrate metabolism and can cause hypoglycaemia as well as weight gain. Strong lagers are often advertised as being suitable for people with diabetes because of their low-carbohydrate content, but the fact that they make you more drunk more quickly outweighs any possible benefit.

Measuring Metabolic Control

A number of laboratory tests have been developed to indicate metabolic control over different time spans. The most commonly used is the measurement of glycosylated haemoglobin (HbA_1). During the life of a red cell, a proportion of haemoglobin combines with glucose. The extent to which this glycosylation occurs is dependent upon the prevailing level of glucose in the blood. The measurement of HbA_1 at a given moment, usually at clinic attendance, will reveal the average blood glucose concentration during the preceding three months.

Self-monitoring of blood glucose (SMBG)

Laboratory tests are helpful, but patients need to know the success or otherwise of their current efforts at blood glucose control. A method of self-monitoring is required that is both simple and accurate. For some patients with Type 2 diabetes, urine testing for glucose may be sufficient and acceptable. For patients with Type 1 diabetes and for insulin-treated patients with Type 2 diabetes, urine testing is too inaccurate, and self-monitoring of blood glucose is necessary if true and immediate feedback is to be obtained. Self-monitoring of blood glucose (SMBG) not only enables the patient to make sensible management decisions, but also gives feedback about the results of recent actions and decisions. It can also be immensely reassuring for patients to know their current blood glucose level, particularly, for instance, before or after vigorous exercise.

SMBG is carried out using small glucose-sensitive reagent strips. The patient obtains a drop of blood by pricking a finger and places the sample on the reagent pad. After a time interval of about one minute, the blood glucose level can be assessed by observing the colour change in the reagent pad. Alternatively, the strip can be placed in a reflectance meter; a pocket-sized electronic device that 'reads' the colour change and displays the blood glucose level numerically. Sophisticated meters are available containing memory chips that can store and display a series of results. Average scores, ranges and extremes of glycaemic levels can be calculated automatically.

For patients who are prepared to self-monitor several times a day for extended periods, there is little doubt that impressive improvements in glycaemic control can be achieved. However, the method has not resulted in the improvements in control that it seemed to promise. One reason for this is that we do not know how often a patient needs to self-monitor to achieve improvements in control. Another is that patients often do not have the necessary skills to execute the technique accurately and reliably, nor the knowledge to translate the results into effective changes to the management regimen.

Not all the problems, however, are caused by errors of performance. Errors of reporting also occur. In other words, the records that patients keep of their SMBG results, written in a log book they bring to clinic, often show large discrepancies when compared with objective records obtained from the data stored in the memory chips. Up to 40 per cent of log-book entries are totally fictitious, others are reported incorrectly to obscure hypo- and hyper-glycaemia and some test results are not written up at all (Shillitoe, 1988). All this has been revealed by secretly fitting meters with memory chips unbeknown to the patient. This has been reported in the journals on many occasions with many different patient populations, including adults, children and pregnant women, even though the latter are generally regarded as being highly compliant. The words used to describe the findings vary from the fairly neutral 'editing' to the much more negative 'deceit'.

These studies made a great impact in diabetes circles, partly because of ethical problems concerning secret recordings, and partly because of the extent of the mismatch between written records kept by patients and the electronic records stored in the meters. From a purely practical point of view, any changes to the regimen based on inaccurate technique or inaccurate reporting may be inappropriate. From a psychological point of view, the dangers are less immediate, but fundamental to the atmosphere in which care is delivered. The main danger is that the consultation becomes 'a kind of trial for the patient in which he or she is held to be accountable for their reactions' (Armstrong, 1991). How easy it is to turn patients from being the innocent victims of an unfortunate disease into liars and deceivers. How easy it is for mistrust, disbelief and scepticism to enter the therapeutic relationship.

Armstrong went on to propose an alternative, more productive, way of looking at the situation:

> . . . *rather than see a discrepancy between glucometer and patients' report as an instance of the patient 'lying', it is equally possible to explore the mismatch as revealing some truth about the way the patient is coping with the illness. Thus, the technology speaks one truth (about the patient's biochemistry) and the patient speaks another about his or her experience of the illness.*

In other words, the mismatch can become the starting-point for an attempt to reach a better understanding of the patients' perceptions, rather than a simple dismissal of the patients' actions and reports. However, as with the story of human insulin, the introduction of reflectance meters has resulted in a devaluation of the importance of the patients' experience, causing an imbalance in care; the placing of a greater reliance upon the technology of care rather than upon the person who has the disease.

Concluding Remarks

The demands made by the regimen are many and varied. This is particularly true for patients who require insulin. What this actually means is changes not just in major areas of life but also in the smaller day-to-day and minute-by-minute niggles and intrusions. These ensure that diabetes is never far from a patient's thoughts. It is always there to intrude and complicate even the simplest aspects of life. Perhaps the best way to bring this home is to close this chapter by quoting this cry from the heart, from Shillitoe (1991):

> *'They say that, if you have to have a chronic disease, diabetes is the one to go for. I was told that I should be able to continue with my normal lifestyle, and that the treatment would be designed around that.*
>
> *Nowadays, I have to give myself four injections each day. I prick my finger and test my blood sugar before each meal and at other times if I feel peculiar. Whenever I go out, I carry an identification card in my purse, and sugar lumps, syringe, blood-letting device and blood-testing strips in my bag.*

I have to reapply for my driving licence every three years, and I have my insurance loaded. I daren't skip a meal. I eat a high-carbohydrate low-fat diet, and try to persuade my family to do the same. I can't get cross and snap at my husband without him accusing me of being hypoglycaemic, and forcing food upon me. If the children are ill or just come home feeling thirsty, my heart races and I worry that I've passed diabetes on to them. I worry about their future, and about mine as well.

When my husband is away on business, I still have my diabetes to keep me company. When we go on holiday, my diabetes comes too.

Now, what was that about leading a normal lifestyle?'

This provides an ideal link to the next chapter, which is about living with diabetes.

Summary

❑ Diabetes is a disorder of the mechanisms that regulate the storage and usage of the energy derived from food. It affects between one and three per cent of the population.

❑ There are two main types of diabetes:

– Type 1 diabetes is a disorder resulting in the destruction of the insulin-producing cells of the pancreas. It most commonly presents in early adolescence.

– Type 2 diabetes is a disorder of insulin-producing cells and there is also tissue resistance to insulin. It most commonly occurs in mid-and late life. About 75% of all patients with diabetes have the Type 2 disorder.

❑ Long-term complications include microvascular degeneration in the eyes, kidneys and nerves, and macrovascular disease affecting the heart and peripheral blood vessels.

❑ Technology plays an important part in the management of diabetes. Reflectance meters and infusion pumps can be helpful additions to a treatment programme, but can give the misleading impression that the technology, not the patient, is responsible for disease control.

❑ People with diabetes have to make many changes in their lifestyle. They will be prescribed a diet and may require tablets or insulin injections as well. They will have to monitor their blood or urine glucose levels regularly, and will be encouraged to lead a healthy lifestyle.

❑ Hypoglycaemia is a common complication of insulin treatment. It is more likely to occur the more strenuously good glucose control is sought.

❑ Modern treatment methods are effective and, if carried out, will result in improved health outcomes. In particular, the dangers of long-term complications can be reduced.

❑ Modern regimens can be very demanding. Not all patients will be able, or will choose, to participate in intensive regimens.

❑ When designing a treatment programme, such things as cultural factors, family circumstances and the patient's lifestyle should be taken into consideration.

❑ Treat the person, not the disease.

3

Living with Diabetes: a Whole New Way of Life

'The main thing I remember about being told the diagnosis was an overwhelming sense of relief. At last I had reasons and explanations for feeling so terrible. Talking to the consultant, I remember feeling immensely reassured that he could explain all my symptoms. Looking back, I am amazed at all the false explanations I had come up with for the way I had been feeling for the couple of months before going to my GP. The muscle cramps I had put down to being unfit, and the skin troubles to poor diet. I had no energy and felt depressed all the time. This I had put down to having just become a father for the first time and having difficulty in adjusting to my new responsibilities. I had given up smoking a few months before, and when I developed an unquenchable thirst, I assumed that I had exchanged one oral addiction for another! What a relief to discover that, far from being unfit, inadequate and neurotic, I was merely diabetic.'

You might think it strange that I start a chapter on living with diabetes with a passage that says that diagnosis can be a positive experience having closed the previous one with a passage describing the daily problems of living with the disease. I do so for two reasons. The first is to illustrate the range of responses that you will meet. The second is to illustrate the importance of understanding what is happening to you; of having convincing explanations for your experiences. To this person, the diagnosis of diabetes was a positive event because it meant that he was psychologically (if not physically) healthy. Other people will react very differently. Each person's experience of diabetes is unique, personal and valid.

Given that there is such a diversity of reactions, what determines how someone will respond to a major upheaval such as the development of diabetes? How will they try to make sense of their experiences? In this chapter I shall try to answer these questions and give you some insight into what it is like to live with diabetes, both as a patient and as a person living closely to someone with the disease.

This is intended to be primarily a practical book, not an academic text, so I am not going to give you lengthy theoretical analyses of the stages of adaptation, of family dynamics or detailed explanations of psychological processes. There are many excellent books that will give you the relevant information should you require it (Broome, 1989; Eiser, 1985). Instead, I shall try to let patients and their families speak for themselves about their own experiences. It might be helpful, however, if I say a few words first about how people generally try to make sense of their experiences.

The Search for Personal Meaning

Even at the best of times the world is a complex and confusing place. Out of the potential chaos, people struggle to make sense of what is happening and to introduce a sense of order and predictability. They do this by generating beliefs, explanations and hypotheses about themselves and their world.

Unless you are ill, you probably think of yourself as being healthy. This is a powerful belief because it helps define your general lifestyle and your day-to-day actions. Being healthy will imply a large number of things: that career choice is open and unrestricted; that meals can be taken at any time, (or skipped, or over-indulged) and that things can be done on impulse with no need for planning or preparation. The importance placed on each aspect, and the exact meanings given to them will vary from person to person, but it is likely that the sort of meanings I have just outlined will be shared by most people. When 'healthy' has to be replaced by 'diabetic', all such expectations have to be re-examined. From freedom to restriction, from healthy to diseased, from certainty to uncertainty; the changes are fundamental, broad-reaching and lifelong.

When healthy people think of ill-health, they tend to think in terms of acute or short-term disorders. That is, that the symptoms will be present for a while, and recovery will then follow. Recovery will occur either because of some treatment that has been taken, or simply because the condition has cleared up. This corresponds to our most common experiences of illness: we feel unwell, we stay off work or school for a few days, then we recover and life returns to normal. This view of illness as being acute and curable is clearly inappropriate for diabetes, as this patient, aged 10½, stated:

'I had to learn so many things, like a complete new way of life. I had to learn my new diet, I had to learn how to inject myself, and test my urine and my blood. I thought I only had to do all those tests, etc., whilst I was in hospital. I didn't realise I had to do them for the rest of my life.'
    (Patient aged 10½, *Archives of Disease in Childhood*, 1984, *59*, 918)

Understanding such changes and accepting the need for them is difficult. Major changes are threatening, and, therefore, unwelcome. They may actually be resisted because they require wide-ranging changes in our picture of ourselves. This is because our explanations and beliefs provide us with structure and stability, like the guy-ropes of a tent. The diagnosis of diabetes is like having all your guy-ropes cut at night while you are sound asleep; you wake with a start, you are disorientated, you flounder about in the dark, the tent is formless, the fabric flimsy and yielding and you have difficulty in finding your way out. Eventually, however, dawn begins to break. You survey the wreckage and you learn how to splice up some new guy-ropes. In a similar fashion, the person with diabetes makes new beliefs and explanations after the old ones have collapsed. Their personal world gradually assumes a new structure and a new form. Although there will be similarities and continuities, it will no longer be the old familiar world, but it is one that can, in time, become robust and stable.

Finding a personal meaning to diabetes

What is the most important thing about living with diabetes? Is it living the good life, now, regardless of the consequences? Is it, perhaps, long-term risk reduction, in terms of avoiding complications; or is it short-term risk reduction, in terms of avoiding a hypoglycaemic reaction while swimming for the school team, or in the middle of your first sexual experience? Is it to do with throwing away your identity bracelet because it makes you feel different to your friends and is a constant, visible, reminder of that difference? It can be all of these things, and much else besides, because values and priorities are not static. They are in a state of constant change as patients continue the lifelong struggle with the disease, and try to adapt to the demands of the moment as well as the demands of the distant future.

Each patient has to find his or her own individual meaning to diabetes. The meaning is personal and you cannot assume that what is important to one person will have any relevance to another. To illustrate this point, Anderson (1986) gave the example of avoiding foods that are high in sugar. To one person this might suggest 'controlling my diabetes' and is therefore a positive act. To another person it might imply 'giving up my favourite foods', and is therefore seen as deprivation. To a third person – or, to the same person at different times or under different circumstances – it might have elements of both.

The meaning that a patient gives to diabetes is determined by a number of factors. If I make the observation that a person does not exist in isolation but is a part of a wider family, social and cultural environment, it is not a profound or original remark, but it is one of fundamental importance. Similarly, nearly all new patients will have some pre-existing ideas about diabetes, however vague or erroneous. All of these will help determine their response to their new situation.

Social and cultural factors. Patients who come to you with different backgrounds to your own may well have beliefs concerning health and illness that are very different to yours. The place of food in society provides a good example. In Mediterranean societies, a woman's identity within her family and her self-esteem come to a large extent from her reputation as a good cook. Plumpness is associated with healthiness and a large appetite is regarded as normal. Given such a background, dietary control, especially if weight loss is recommended, will present particular difficulties. Patients from some Asian societies may not regard the dietary management of diabetes as 'proper' treatment. Further, great emphasis may be placed on maintaining dietary traditions. This may involve communal cooking and the giving and eating of sweetmeats as expressions of hospitality. Patients may seek advice from traditional healers and take traditional remedies. Even within ethnic or social groups, different people will place different emphases on the importance of healthy eating and even upon the importance of good health itself.

Existing knowledge of diabetes. Most members of the general population know at least something of diabetes. This may be as a result of national or local health promotion campaigns, or through seeing the array of 'diabetic' chocolate and jams in food stores. It may be because they have a family member, or perhaps a friend or colleague, with diabetes.

These prior experiences create expectations in the mind of new patients about what lies in store for them. These expectations are often negative and frightening. Because charities have to raise money, their fund-raising appeals are often emotive ones that emphasize the distressing side of diabetes; hence the heart-wrenching picture of a young child giving herself an injection while her worried mother looks on that featured in a recent advertising campaign by a national diabetes organization. Similarly, because the blood glucose control of many patients was poor in the past and treatment methods less successful, new patients may remember the struggles of older relatives and the traumas of disabling and painful complications and believe that the same fate awaits them:

> *'Because my father had diabetes, I had already spent years in fear of getting it. His fears and anxieties, his trials and tribulations of living with the disease now dominated my thoughts. The terror I connected with the very word diabetes had to be dispelled . . . Memories sprang up, minute to minute, in particular remembering my father taking injections. In my mind I saw his insulin reactions. I saw the different person he became when his blood sugar would swing too low, and I saw the changes he had to make because of the diabetes. Never did I think of how normal was his life with diabetes. No, I concentrated only on the bad. It was a relief to dump the whole mess in the doctor's hands.'*

> (Schwartz, 1988)

Contrast this with the account given at the start of the chapter. There is no sense of relief here. Instead, because this patient had distressing memories of a parent with diabetes, his expectations about it were terrifying and threatening. This led him to expect that his own diabetes would cause him major problems. So powerful were these feelings that, in the short-term, the only way he could cope with them was by temporarily passing all responsibility to the doctor.

Personal experiences and memories can have a profound and lasting effect. I remember a middle-aged woman who had developed Type 1 diabetes as a teenager. When she told her mother, her shocked response was: 'Diabetics always die young.' These words had stayed with the patient, and whenever she decided to work hard to achieve good control, they came back to haunt her: what is the point of good control to prevent future problems if there is no future? You can see how her mother's words, although very wrong, helped form her defeatist attitude.

Why me? Why now? Following diagnosis, people search for a cause for their disease and try to understand what is happening to them. Quite often an apparent cause is found in an incident that occurred just before the onset. Lindsay (1985) gave a number of examples of the explanations offered by youngsters. She cited a ten-year-old who saw the onset of her diabetes two years earlier as the result of taking money from her sister's money-box to buy sweets. To construe diabetes as a punishment for a misdemeanour in this manner is likely to have profound and far-reaching effects on self-esteem, social and academic performance and other aspects of personal functioning. Adults, who have a more sophisticated understanding of disease processes, are less likely to draw such obviously wrong conclusions, but you cannot afford to assume that this is always necessarily so. Remember the man at the start of the chapter? He had very clear explanations in terms of parenthood, lack of fitness and so on, all of which were incorrect.

Sharing a perspective

I have already raised the question of what patients regard as being of importance about diabetes. I suggested a range of answers, from living the good life now regardless of the future, to making every effort to control blood glucose in order to prevent future health difficulties. As a health worker, you will naturally lean heavily towards the second alternative, and you will try to influence patients to share your perspective. This is because during your training you have been taught to value scientific medicine and the importance of good health. Your daily working environment reinforces this. On the other hand, a patient's perspective and environment might be very different.

Your perspective will probably differ from the patient's in a number of ways and you might be unaware of this. For instance, if someone is experiencing a period of poor control, physicians have a tendency to regard this as being more foreseeable (and, by implication, more preventable) than the patient. Additionally, and perhaps understandably, physicians are more likely to give the credit for good control to the success of the treatment while seeing problems as being less to do with the treatment and more to do with the patient. You can probably think of examples from your own clinical experience of the sort of differences in perspective that can commonly occur. I remember one patient whose problems with her weight were simply put down to not following her diet. To the patient, however, the problem was one of unhappy home circumstances, and her inability to keep to the diet was just a symptom of this.

I am not singling out the medical profession for special criticism. Comparable studies have yet to be performed with members of other helping professions. However, I have no reason to suppose that the findings would be very different wherever the spotlight was trained.

I shall repeatedly return to the importance of understanding the patient's own perspective, rather than assuming that it is the same as yours. I shall deal with practical ways of doing this later. My point at the moment is that a passion for regular exercise and an enthusiasm for the glycaemic index may be totally at odds with the patient's own experience of their disease, and what they regard as important in actually living their lives.

Living with Diabetes

We approach a particular situation armed with our existing beliefs and expectations, and we experience it in the light of them. According to the nature of the situation and the appropriateness of the beliefs, they will either be confirmed or confounded and in some way modified. If we meet a similar situation again, they will undergo further refinement.

Any events that occur during a lifetime of diabetes can, potentially, require further adjustments. They will cause a personal disturbance insofar as they require a reappraisal of ideas about oneself, one's activities and one's future plans.

Suppose, for example, that as a patient with diabetes you have come to think of yourself as being in control of your disease. I do not mean control in the limited sense of blood glucose regulation, but in the broader sense of being in charge of it, of feeling that you have mastery over it. That makes you feel good about yourself. You have the confidence to do what you want to do. Diabetes, while a continuing presence in your life, does not tower above it. Then one day, quite out of the blue, you experience a major hypoglycaemic attack at work; one moment you are going about your duties, the next you are sitting dazed and confused in a strange office trying to convince some ambulance officers that there is no need to be taken to the local casualty department.

What does this do to your beliefs about yourself, your self-confidence, your dignity and your feelings of being in control? Almost certainly, you will reflect upon what happened. You might think about what you could have done differently that day; you might plan to do things differently in future; you might experience feelings of embarrassment and, perhaps, twinges of fear. You might discuss these things with your family or with clinic staff in your efforts to understand what happened and why it happened. If you are fortunate, you will find reasons that are not too damaging to your beliefs about yourself or too distressing in their implications, for example, 'I got up late that morning and I was in a rush; I couldn't remember taking my insulin; I think I must have had it twice. I'll just have to be more careful in future'. If you are less fortunate, the implications might be more fundamental, for example, 'I got hardly any warning symptoms. My nervous system must be degenerating. It could happen again at any time'. Life changes and life goes on in a constant process of adjustment and readjustment. Here are some more examples of peoples' experiences of diabetes. I have chosen them because they illustrate something important about living with the disease.

Children and young people

'When it was time for me to go back to school, I did not want to go back ... My Mum tried to make me go but I decided to run away instead. I also felt that I wanted to die. I ran out the front door and walked around just thinking about myself. I thought that my Mum did not care about me and that nobody cared about me. I decided to go home as I nearly got lost. When I got home my Mum had asked the health visitor to come and see me. I was rude to the health visitor and my Mum as I felt they were being cruel to me. Afterwards when I had calmed down, I was very ashamed of myself, and I went back to school in the afternoon and I enjoyed myself.'
(Patient aged 10½, *Archives of Disease in Childhood*, 1984, 59, 918)

This young person was describing the turmoil she felt following diagnosis. Her description is characteristic of a person in crisis: anxiety, disorganization, self-doubt and hostility. Everyone is at fault: herself, her mother and the health visitor who is trying to help her. The issues that she faces – getting on with normal daily life, learning to live with diabetes, her emotional reactions – are those that face all newly diagnosed patients. She will face them every day of her life but she will discover ways of reducing their impact and their immediacy. Some of this she will do on her own, some of it with the support of her family and some of it with the support of clinic staff.

Effects on parents. Parents may react with shock and disbelief. The struggle for parents to understand what has happened is difficult. The search for a reason may result in self-blame:

'I think we have now lost our sense of guilt at the fact that Max is diabetic. When he was first diagnosed our early response was in the following terms: Is it my fault? If we had noticed the listlessness and the heavy drinking earlier,

could something have been done to prevent the condition? If I had known, I would not have shouted at him for wetting himself.'

(Thomas, 1984)

Even the most ordinary of activities become fraught with uncertainty:

'When he came home, I can remember it was like having a new baby in the house. Every so often, we would find an excuse for checking to see if he was alright. At night we left his bedroom door open and we did not sleep at all well.'

(Thomas, 1984)

The realities of coping with diabetes unfold as the months and years roll by. The shock of diagnosis and initial worries fade with time, familiarity and experience and as confidence is built up. Although some fears become less intense, others remain and are never far away:

'Nothing terrible ever happened, but there was always a gnawing fear that it might. If we went out for the evening, the baby sitter had a list of all the numbers to call in an emergency, a box of biscuits, sweet drinks, everything. But where ever we went I still couldn't really settle. I kept thinking will she know what to do if he goes "hypo"? When he went on trips with the school it was the same – will the teachers know what to do and how to bring him round? If he was late home from school, I was on tenterhooks until he got back. When he did get back I was always so relieved to see him, but it never came out as relief, more as irritation and exasperation. He must have thought that I didn't trust him, but I did. It was my own feelings I couldn't cope with very well. It didn't really stop until after he had gone to college. It gradually sunk in that he had become an adult, it was his life and there was nothing I could do anymore.'

(Thomas, 1984)

It is a challenge for parents to learn how to give support and encouragement without appearing to be intrusive on the one hand or uncaring on the other. Part of the challenge is for them to learn to live with their own feelings as well as those of their child. Sometimes, changes and insights occur very slowly. Sometimes, it is only when you look back in time that you realize what was really happening.

Effects on family members. The needs of the family member with diabetes have to be balanced against the needs of all the other members of the family. Everyone has to adapt and accommodate. Take the question of dietary restrictions. As a parent, you can either give your child a special diet and run the risk of making him or her feel different, or you can try to change the eating habits of all the family.

This, too, it not without its risks. The rather forthright twelve-year-old sister of a teenage patient said this:

> *'I can't even have bacon and eggs now, Mum's gone and hidden the frying pan in the attic; and I hate brown toast. Dad hates brown toast too, he's always saying so.'*
> (Lindsay, 1985)

Notice how the last sentence seems to indicate some undercurrents of discontent within the family as a whole.

Adults

Frustration and uncertainty. Living with uncertainty is difficult. It can be like fighting fog. Situations sometimes arise that make patients feel helpless and powerless:

> *'I blotted the blood from the testing strip and took one look at it. Deep orange. Again. I could feel my chest begin to tighten and my jaws begin to clench. What had I done wrong this time?'*

There are always limits to what can be achieved and what can be controlled. Defining those limits and discovering where they lie is important for any patient. Knowing what you can do and what you cannot gives you the boundaries within which you can exert control. The trouble is, the boundaries keep changing.

Hypoglycaemia. The loss of control, both physical and emotional, that accompanies low blood glucose is a powerful and unpleasant experience that most patients try hard to avoid, not always with the desired results:

> *'I remember the time I went to stay with my girlfriend's parents for the first time. We went out for a proper meal with them and I really wanted to make a good impression. They knew I was diabetic but there was no way I was going to let that get in the way. The last thing that was going to happen was that I was going to go hypo if we had to wait to be served or anything like that. So I cut back on the insulin. During the meal I felt on edge. I wasn't sure whether that was nerves or low blood sugar, so I kept nibbling bits of bread and things all the time. Next morning my blood sugar was about one million, so I took loads of extra insulin. I passed out about lunchtime. That was when she learned how to mix up a glucagon injection.'*

Reliance on others. Diabetes often brings to the surface issues of independence and autonomy:

> *'I rely a lot on my wife for all the cooking and meal planning. I'd be lost without her. I'm grateful it didn't happen until all the children were grown up and settled. I don't like to think about the future, especially if anything happened to my wife, but I suppose I'd get by. I'd have to, wouldn't I?'*

Despite worries about the future, this patient, like the one in the previous example, finds comfort in positive thinking. In this case, it is the fact that the family had left home before he became unwell. There is a mixture of resignation and defiance in the statement that, if the worst came to the worst, he would just have to get on with it. He would not relish the situation, but he would cope with it.

Living with complications. The development of degenerative changes presents a real threat to the coping strategies that have been developed over the years of having diabetes. For the person who has valued good metabolic control and who has striven to avoid complications, their efforts have been in vain. On the other hand, to the patient who has been less diligent in self-care and who has trusted to luck for long-term good health, it may seem that the price is now being paid for the years of self-neglect.

As with other times of change and crisis, strong emotions can be expected. Some may react with feelings of hopelessness, and be tempted to abandon all attempts at self-care ('What's the point, it never helped me anyway'); others may feel guilt and remorse ('I never took enough care of myself, I suppose I've got what I deserved'); others will feel resentful and angry ('Lots of other people had no better control than I did, so why has it happened to me?'); and some may question the competence of their helpers:

> *'I had my eyes checked every year, so why couldn't the ophthalmologist have seen the retinal bleeding coming? Why can't they do more for me now that it's happened? I ask my doctor if I'm going blind but all he says is we'll have to wait and see. Wait and see! I ask you! What a thing to say!'*

Some will find their self-esteem and sense of personal worth seriously undermined ('If I can't do my job any more, what's left in my life?'). Many will experience a combination of these powerful and disturbing feelings. Many will move beyond this and find a source of peace and pride in coping with pain and other discomforts, such as visual impairment:

'You know, I have become much more positive in my way of thinking since I had complications. I am much more grateful now, for what I have left. I put a value on that I can see, every day. So, I am actually grateful, and sometimes it is difficult to be with people who are well, and they . . . they have no sense of being grateful that they are so well off.'

(Ternulf Nyhlin, 1990)

Partners' Perspectives

Diabetes has an impact upon personal relationships. I asked the wife of a patient how diabetes had affected her:

'Has any good come of it? Perhaps it makes you more appreciative of the things you have still got. He still feels very well. In fact, he's very healthy apart from the diabetes.

What's the worst part? I suppose its the constant uncertainty. If he's late home I worry, especially if it's dark and the roads are bad. Yes, I worry about the future and whether he'll escape complications. It's all very well the doctors saying the risks are small, but the risks of him getting diabetes in the first place must have been small too so I'm bound to worry.

I don't like the regularity. Life is controlled by mealtimes. It doesn't bother me so much now I've got used to it, but its a bind always having to plan ahead. Hypos frighten me. I don't like the way his personality seems to change. He gets so stubborn and aggressive. So far – touch wood – he's never lost consciousness but that's something I always worry about. Thank goodness he gets good warning symptoms.

How do I cope? It's never far away but I try and push it away and carry on as normal. If he wasn't diabetic perhaps I'd worry about something else. I just think that something could have happened to either of us at any time. It could have been a lot worse. If it had happened fifty years ago before they discovered insulin he'd be dead by now. All you can do is be sensible and eat a healthy diet. That's not so bad, is it?'

She has had to make changes to her own way of life. She has had to cope with worry and uncertainty. She finds strength from reminding herself of positive things, from finding something good to say, despite the problems. She puts a positive interpretation on the difficulties and this helps her to contain them.

Concluding Remarks

I am struck by the ability patients have of making life meaningful in spite of difficulties. I have a sense of privilege in being allowed to talk to patients and to learn from them how they cope, how they find a balance between the demands of diabetes and their own personal needs. This is seldom easy and is seldom accomplished without a fight. As a helper, you may be called upon to provide understanding, information, practical support and emotional support at different times. These may be required not only by patients, but by family members as well. These are comprehensive demands. In the following chapters I shall try to give you the knowledge and the skills that you will need to meet them.

Summary

❑ Throughout life, people try to make sense of their experiences. They develop ways of looking at the world and of interpreting it to make it understandable and predictable.

❑ The patient's ways of looking at health and illness may be very different to your own.

❑ The diagnosis of diabetes is usually a traumatic event. This is because many of the fundamental concepts that people hold dear about themselves have been rendered inappropriate or irrelevant. Other things that affect how a person reacts to the diagnosis include:

− their previous personal or family experiences of diabetes;
− their knowledge of diabetes;
− their self-concept and self-esteem.

❑ Once diabetes has been developed, the patient and the immediate family have a number of tasks to perform. These include resuming normal daily life, learning to live with the disease, and achieving an emotional balance. The greater the changes that are required, the harder adaptation is likely to be.

❑ The process of understanding, changing and adapting never ceases.

4

The Helping Relationship

The helping relationship is the setting in which patients express their needs and concerns, and in which helpers bring their technical expertise and psychological skills to bear. The relationship is used to facilitate both good psychological and physical care. In fact, it is more accurate to say that rather than just being the setting for good quality care, the relationship is itself a significant part of the care process. In this chapter I shall discuss the components of the helping relationship and the skills of relationship building that the helper needs in order to foster it.

Compliance or Empowerment? Two Contrasting Views

How best to sum up the nature of the relationship you should strive for? Is it one in which you are the expert and expect patients to comply with your instructions, or is it a partnership in which you both work together to achieve certain goals? One of the things that often puzzles and annoys helpers is that they spend a great deal of time and effort devising suitable diets, working out insulin regimens, and promoting healthy living, only to have patients go away and do none of it, or perhaps very little. In other words, patients often do not comply with carefully formulated treatment plans. There are many reasons why this is so, and one of the most important is the nature of the relationship between helper and patient.

Compliance

The word 'compliance' has overtones of doing as you are told; of obeying orders. It assumes that health workers, because of their training and expertise, know what is best for patients, and it follows from this that patients have a duty and an obligation to follow the advice once given. To speak of compliance is to help create and perpetuate an atmosphere in which the powerful clinician gives orders to a submissive patient. If patients vote with their feet and stop attending the clinic, they are said to have 'defaulted', a word which, like non-compliance, puts responsibility and blame firmly on their shoulders.

Patients, however, are at perfect liberty to reject your advice – and a good many will, even though they might not tell you. In practice, health workers find this independence difficult to stomach. It is illuminating to compare this attitude with that of professionals in other occupations:

> *'Not every bit of advice given by solicitors, architects, business consultants and other professionals is followed by those who have sought their services. Clients exercise their judgement, as is their right, when presented with professional advice even though they may not have the professional expertise claimed by their advisors. They are capable of healthy scepticism, of balancing advice from different sources, and of requiring supportive evidence. Clients' failure to follow advice may have serious consequences, yet these professions tend to see this independence as part of clients' rights and if they study non-compliance at all, do not do so in terms of client deficiency but in terms of necessary improvements in the services they offer.'*
>
> (Thompson, 1984)

As helpers in health care, we have a long way to go before we feel comfortable when patients exercise their autonomy. We do, of course, have a long tradition to contend with, dating back at least as far as Hippocrates, who wrote: 'Keep a watch also on the faults of the patients, which often make them lie about the taking of things prescribed.' Whole-person care is difficult in such a background of distrust and suspicion as patients may feel devalued and unmotivated.

Empowerment

Many people take issue with the term 'compliance' for the reasons just discussed, but particularly because it places too much emphasis on the helper's role as an expert who determines what the patient should or should not do. The term 'adherence' is sometimes used, as it seems to imply a more active willingness on the part of the patient to follow the recommendations. Words such as 'co-operation' and 'collaboration' suggest the same thing. Others prefer to talk about a 'treatment alliance' being forged between the patient and the helper, who then work in partnership. This takes the idea of the patient as participant a stage further. The ultimate extension of this is to think in terms of 'empowerment': giving patients the skills, the knowledge and, therefore, the power, to enable them to play a leading part in their own management.

As we saw in Chapter Two, modern treatment programmes can be very demanding and carry risks in their own right. Who, other than the patient, has the right or the authority to make such decisions? Even if research studies have established that a particular treatment is of proven value, individuals may decide that for them the costs are excessive and too high a price to pay for the potential benefit. The costs, of course, are measured in emotional, psychological and social terms as well as physical and financial ones. As human beings, patients have the right to make the major decisions about their lives, including decisions about management. When working in partnership, the member of staff helps the patient to make informed choices for themselves about their self-care.

Gibson (1991) summarized the main beliefs that underlie the empowerment view in the following terms.

1. Health belongs to the individual. The individual has the prime responsibility for his or her own health. Although helpers have a responsibility to promote health, they do not have a monopoly on it.

2. The individual's capacity for growth and self-determination needs to be respected. Patients have the ability to make decisions and act on their own behalf, although they may need information and help to do so.

3. Helpers cannot empower people; they can only empower themselves. However, helpers can enable them to develop, secure and use resources that will promote a sense of control and self-efficacy.

4. Helpers need to value patients' participation and be prepared to accept that patients will make decisions that are different to those that professionals might have made for them. Those who try to help must surrender their need for control as this leads to dependency.

5. There must be mutual respect between helper and patient. The relationship is not one-sided, where one party is viewed as inferior and incompetent relative to the other. Empowerment is a collaborative process.

6. Mutual trust is a necessary condition for empowerment.

These are fine words which many helpers will have no difficulty in endorsing, at least on paper. In reality, however, some will think that talk of empowerment or partnership is no more than pious humbug;

that the power balance is always tilted heavily in favour of the professional; that many people actually want their helpers to take control and to be told what to do for the best; as one patient put it, to 'dump the whole mess in the doctor's hands'. For some, this will be true, but not for others. For those for whom it is true, it may not be so all the time. Some professionals will argue that patients will not be able to understand the finer details of the disease and its management, and that it is unnecessary and futile to attempt to explain them. I believe that patients should at least be offered the opportunity of finding out more about the disease if they wish. Others will argue that because patients on the whole do not ask questions, they do not want to be involved or to hear explanations. I shall suggest later that the non-involvement of patients is a consequence of an attitude among helpers that fosters non-involvement, and that there is some evidence that improving patient's involvement in their care can improve their metabolic control. Others will claim that they do not have the time to engage in a collaborative partnership, but will continue to waste time by asking questions to which they already know the answers, or questions to which there are no answers. Some will persist in giving advice or making recommendations that are so far divorced from the patient's own circumstances that they cannot possibly be followed.

These attitudes are likely to result in a dissatisfied and poorly controlled patient, with whom more time has to be spent as more frequent appointments will be necessary. The benefits from attempts to empower patients and families include a positive self-concept, increased personal satisfaction, self-efficacy, a sense of mastery and control, justice (in that their choices have been respected) and improved quality of life. Whatever words you use to describe it – empowerment, partnership, or whole-person care – it makes good human, clinical and economic sense.

I have examined these contrasting views of helping at some length because the assumptions we each make about our activities are often unspoken. It is helpful to think them through and to decide where you stand because your beliefs help determine how you actually behave. It is also surprisingly easy to think that you believe in partnership, and yet in practice to behave in ways that disempower the patient: the introduction of human insulin is a case in point. This is less likely to happen if you are aware of your underlying beliefs.

As every session with a patient has to take place somewhere, I shall start by examining key features of the location where you do your work.

Location and Physical Surroundings

The surroundings where we work help determine how we work. They lead us to behave in certain ways, and for us to expect patients to behave in certain ways. The location also creates expectations in the minds of patients about the kind of interaction that is about to happen and what sorts of behaviour are acceptable. If you see patients in their own home or at a bedside, the comments in this section will be less relevant for you; you will have to rely more on your communication skills to set the scene for a productive and therapeutic relationship. Wherever possible, however, it makes good sense to make sure as many factors as possible are working in favour of you both.

Think about the place where you normally see patients. Ask yourself:

- If you have a waiting area, how are the space and the furniture arranged? Does the area encourage everyone to sit in glum isolation, leafing through old and dog-eared magazines until their turn comes? If so, what can be done to spruce it up and make it more welcoming?
- What does the condition of your interview room say to someone entering it for the first time? If it is full of clutter, with papers and books everywhere, will they get the impression that your real job is paperwork and that they are intruding on your time and keeping you from your proper work? If, on the other hand, it is very spartan or clinical, it may create the expectation that the session will be short and confined to medical issues.
- Is the room a place where people can feel at ease and be open about themselves? If you have photographs of your happy, loving children on the desk, how do you think this will be received by your childless couples, or by the parents of difficult teenagers?
- Does the room say anything about you that might be better unsaid? What will your patients think when they see photographs on your desk of you looking smug at your graduation ceremony and framed copies of your certificates and diplomas on the walls?
- Is the room appropriate for people in the range of ages that you will be seeing there? Children, teenagers and adults all have different views about the kind of room in which they will feel comfortable.

The room should be as relaxing and inviting as you can make it. There is no need to erase all evidence of your personality, but it is important to be aware of too much individuality showing through if you do not want to alienate too many patients. Try sitting in the chair where the patients usually sit and have a critical look round. Get someone to sit in your own chair and have a conversation with them. Does it feel odd? Are you, literally and metaphorically, looking up to them because you are on a lower chair? Is there a gross disparity in comfort between your chair and the patient's? It is usually possible to make changes, although there will be limits; you cannot do much in the short-term about the physical location of the room, or a noisy environment, except apologize for it. In the longer term you can fight for better accommodation.

You should do your best to avoid introducing status barriers into the room as these create a sense of distance between people. The greater the distance, the less likely patients are to talk freely about their worries or to reveal their emotions. They will think you are too busy or too important to deal with their trivial complaints. They will be too embarrassed to open up to you about their fears and worries. Most people are familiar with common status barriers, such as the helper sitting behind a desk and having a more comfortable chair, but there are many other subtle ways of demonstrating your superiority. Drinking coffee is one, unless you offer a cup to the patient as well. Accepting telephone calls is another; do not do this: it is the patient's time and should be preserved for them alone. Divert the telephone, hang a 'Do Not Disturb' sign on the door and leave your radio-pager with someone else.

Despite your best efforts, however, disturbances are sometimes unavoidable. If you are interrupted, it is helpful to restart the proceedings by briefly recapping the point you had reached before the interruption. This ensures that you are both concentrating on the same thing and back on track again. If you know that you will have to take a telephone call during the session or be interrupted in some other way, it is a good idea to mention this at the start of the session. This is good manners. It is remarkable how tolerant patients are of our behaviour, and it is regrettable how often they need to be.

Issues of status barriers and professional distance are particularly relevant when dealing with young people. This is why some services organize clinics away from health-service premises. Some arrange social gatherings for adolescents in, say, the local bowling-alley, where enjoyment can be mixed with social support and education in real-life situations. Many helpers find this difficult at first, as they can no longer take cover behind a uniform or professional façade. If you take to heart the comments in the next section, this will be less of a problem.

Key Helper Behaviours

The more you are yourself in the sessions, the more you will create an atmosphere in which the patient feels able to be open and honest. The more you hide behind a front of professional detachment, or keep the patient at arm's length, or try to give the impression of being a paragon of virtue or someone who has all the answers, the less likely a therapeutic atmosphere becomes. Such behaviours will make the patient feel inept, inadequate or unworthy.

There are a number of things you should try to do.

Genuineness

Be yourself. If you have ever been a patient yourself, you probably found that you had most confidence in your helpers when you felt that you were dealing with a person, not an impersonal professional front. Try not to hide behind professional anonymity and detachment.

Helpers are tempted to keep their professional distance for a number of reasons. One is self-preservation. You may fear that you will become enmeshed in the patient's problems if you do not maintain your reserve. This is particularly the case for medical staff, who sometimes feel that expressing concern and human feeling will damage their ability to cope with pain and suffering. Their fear is that acknowledging feelings, either their own or those of the patient, will make them vulnerable to overwhelming or painful emotions. Another reason is fear or ignorance; you may worry that you will be asked difficult and awkward questions to which you have no answers, or are uncertain how best to communicate the answers if the patient is likely to find them painful and distressing.

Finally, there is self-importance; some people see the clinic as a stage upon which they play the starring role, while the patient has – for preference – a non-speaking part. You might be immensely important at your work-place, but when you are with patients, this counts for nothing. Park your pretensions with the car; they have no place in the consulting room. Cultivate the habit of carrying an internal monitoring within yourself. If you notice that you are hiding behind your role or being defensive, then pause and think.

Be consistent. If you are being inconsistent, there is a strong chance that you are not being therapeutic. By inconsistent I do not simply mean saying one thing one week and something else the next, or starting a new treatment programme with a great wave of enthusiasm that waxes and wanes as the weeks go by. These are obviously frustrating for the patient who never knows what to expect, or whether it is something they have said or done which is the cause of your instability. There are less obvious ways of being inconsistent. You need to be aware of them and to guard against them. The first is an internal inconsistency; a mismatch between the various components of your behaviour:

Obese patient to dietitian, *'You must get fed up of seeing me each month; I never seem to lose any weight.'*
Dietitian (forcing a thin smile), *'Of course not! That's what I'm here for!'* (thinking, 'You bet I do!', as the frustration wells up inside.)

Here there is a clear gap between feelings, thoughts and the actual words she uses. A response such as, 'It can't be easy for either of us' might have been better. This would have acknowledged the patient's remark and given her the opportunity to follow it up should she wish. A flat denial, which is contradicted by all other aspects of behaviour, simply creates a gulf between the helper and the patient. The helper has not been genuine, and an opportunity to explore the patient's frustrations has been missed.

A second form of inconsistency concerns behaving differently with different patients. Treating patients as individuals and showing respect for their individuality is always highly desirable, but sometimes patients will arouse strong feelings that get in the way of forming a helping relationship:

• Patient A has not been keeping to the diet plan and their blood glucose control is not good. Patient A is physically very attractive, personable and has a winning smile. You seem to have a lot in common. Patient A wants to give up smoking and asks for your help.

• Patient B has not been keeping to the diet either and has equally poor blood glucose control. Patient B has an accent that grates on your ears, and holds political views that are the exact reverse of your own. Your nose tells you that B is unfamiliar with the use of deodorants. Patient B also wants your help in giving up smoking.

Are you tempted, even for a moment, to see Patient A more frequently than B? Are you tempted, just for a second, to produce a greater number of helpful suggestions for A, or to spend more time in discussing the problems of stopping smoking? Are you more understanding of A and more tolerant of lapses? Of course you are. Furthermore, while Patient A is obviously battling hard against tremendous odds and deserves your full support and attention, are you more likely to think that patient B is unmotivated to stop smoking? Of course you are.

Think about the effects that patients have upon you. When they arouse strong feelings, positive in the case of Patient A, or negative as in the case of B, be alert to this and recognize that they can make it difficult to form an appropriate helping relationship.

Be honest. This seems obvious, but it is worth explaining because honesty means a number of things. First, make sure that there are no gaps between what you say and the reality of the situation:

> *'When I was young I remember a doctor forever trying to send me on a holiday for children with diabetes and in the same breath trying to convince me that I was "normal". I could never understand it: if I was just like everyone else, why did I have to go on a special holiday? She never did convince me. In fact, I ended up disrespecting the doctor's views. It was me, not her, who had the condition, yet she was telling me how I was supposed to feel and what I could or couldn't do.'* (Balance, Oct/Nov. 1992, 32.)

Most youngsters have a finely tuned insincerity detector; they can spot deception at a hundred paces. Older patients may be just as perceptive, although they tend not to give voice to such thoughts and feelings quite so readily.

Honesty also means that when patients ask you a question and you do not know the answer, you do not try to bluff your way out, nor do you try and blind them with science. It means that you do not make promises that you cannot keep, nor make commitments you know you cannot meet.

Honesty means correcting any misconceptions that arise. Sometimes patients will tell you what they think you said in previous sessions, and these so-called 'quotations' can be wildly inaccurate. This may result from a simple misunderstanding, or your message may have been transformed into what the patient hoped you might have said. Sometimes you will have no recollection of the previous conversation at all, but it sounds like something you certainly would not have said. Unless you want the misunderstanding to continue, you must address the situation without making the patient feel either dishonest or confused. Avoid disagreements and instead use a phrase such as, 'If I gave that impression then it was a mistake. What I would have meant is . . .'

Be natural. Try to behave naturally and with spontaneity. If you are very hesitant, weighing up what to say and then saying it with all the deliberation and gravity of a politician justifying the latest policy reversal, then your words will also be met with a large measure of disbelief. At the other extreme, verbalizing every thought and saying exactly what you think without tact or sensitivity is equally damaging. This is not what is meant by genuineness. Aim for the middle ground, where tact coexists with directness.

Respect and acceptance

To respect a patient is to believe in their dignity and their right to self-determination, even when they choose to travel down paths that you find difficult to accept or understand. It is demonstrated by your behaviour:

You are driving one evening in a strange part of town, looking for the tennis club. You lose your way, so you pull alongside a pedestrian and wind down your window. With a start, you recognize him as one of your particularly badly controlled patients. You feel embarrassed because you had words with him at clinic earlier in the week; his self-monitoring records were patchy and unreliable, and his HbA, was high. You wanted him to start using a pen injector, but good control did not seem to be important to him and he was not too keen on coming back to clinic for closer 'supervision' (your phrase!) when you wanted him to, in a month's time. However, it is too late to drive on, so you ask for directions. Do you expect him to say:

- *'I'm sorry, I don't give directions to people who drive Volvo estate cars.'*
- *'You would find it a lot easier if you started from the other side of town; I wouldn't start from here if I were you.'*
- *'Surely you don't want to go to the tennis club? Everyone goes bowling nowadays.'*
- *'Move over, I'll drive you there.'*
- *'Turn left at the lights, and it's half a mile along on the right.'*

You would be very surprised if he chose one of the first four alternatives, although he should, if he takes a leaf out of your book and models his responses on your recent behaviour to him at the clinic. In fact, of course, he is highly unlikely to query your destination, your route, or your choice of vehicle. He will respect your decisions and will almost certainly tell you what you want to know. I realize that the role-reversal is not exact (at least he does not ask you to come back next month and tell him if you won your match), but I hope my point is clear. It is easy to make assumptions and personal judgements about patients, their character and behaviour. It is easy to disapprove and condemn. When you do, barriers will be erected that get in the way of open communication.

Respect is transmitted through:

- actions that protect a patient's dignity and privacy;
- listening to what patients are saying;
- trying to help patients mobilize their own resources;
- explaining procedures and actions before carrying them out;
- giving patients choices wherever possible.

Ask yourself a number of questions: 'Do I consider the patient's wishes when planning a care programme? Is my treatment of the patient dependent upon who they are, or what I think of them, rather than upon what they need?' When you do this, the benefits are clear. This is what one mother wrote about the open respectful approach taken by staff when her teenage daughter developed diabetes:

It was almost as if she were the leader of a team dedicated to her future well-being in which to a large extent she voluntarily made the important decisions . . . she lost part of her childhood but gained a strength and determination that she applies to most areas of her life now. It was the very open and kindly approach by the staff that helped to support her at this time.

If you openly disapprove of what the patient says or does, or fail to show an interest in issues that the patient regards as important, you are offering only limited and conditional acceptance. The quality of the helping relationship will be diminished.

Self-awareness. Respect and acceptance are easy when the patient is similar to you and when blood glucose control is excellent. It becomes progressively harder the more unlike each other you become and the more their self-care deviates from what you think it ought to be. Ask yourself, 'Is my acceptance of this patient based on their HbA_1 values?' and, 'Is it based on their similarity to me?'

To accept patients for who they are we need to know something of who we are. We need a certain amount of self-knowledge and self-confidence. We also have to be able to put that knowledge into practice. This can be difficult because we are all subject to group and cultural pressures to think in certain ways or to adopt certain viewpoints. To know what we truly feel means to be aware of these forces. When I teach counselling skills on the local course in diabetes nursing for nurses and midwives, one of the topics we cover is acceptance, and the way in which we do this is by discussing clinical vignettes. This one is based on an exercise given in Nelson-Jones (1983). What feelings and reactions does it arouse in you?

Khalid has diabetes. He is a 23-year-old gay man who is leading a promiscuous life based on finding partners in gay clubs and bars. He has taken several overdoses in the past year since the older man with whom he had been living ended the relationship.

As you can imagine, this example brings out racial, sexual and mental illness stereotypes and prejudices. The problem that we as helpers have to face is not just identifying the feelings, but also admitting them, even to ourselves, and making sure that our behaviour with the patient is not influenced adversely by them. If we discuss our feelings about Khalid at the beginning of a course, everyone is very concerned to say all the correct things, such as; 'No, of course I would treat Khalid exactly like any other patient. I might talk to him about safe sex, but apart from that he is no different to any one else; some of my best friends . . .' If we hold the session later, however, when the group has gelled, the discussion is quite different. Participants are much more relaxed and prepared to talk openly about the ways in which their feelings about race, homosexuality and self-harm might get in the way of forming a helping relationship. We can then explore how this might happen through feelings of revulsion or compassion, or perhaps by making extra special allowances to demonstrate that you are not prejudiced.

We are not blank sheets of paper for the patient to write upon, nor should we aspire to be. We have biases and prejudices and there is a limit to our neutrality. Acceptance and respect do not mean having no feelings of your own, no viewpoints and no biases. They do mean identifying them in yourself, recognizing them when they occur and making sure that their expression and influence are contained. You can do this by noticing when these things happen, and when they do, asking yourself what is it that makes you react in that way.

Empathy

Empathy is an important means for understanding patients and informing them that they are understood. It involves trying to see the world through their eyes, but without losing your sense of objectivity. It means a certain amount of identification with what the patient is feeling and saying while retaining a degree of detachment so you do not become immersed and biased. To show empathy means that the helper has understood what the patient is feeling or expressing and has communicated that understanding.

In some ways empathy is similar to other responses, such as sympathy and compassion. These are natural and valuable emotions, signalling that you accept the patient's state and providing comfort, but they differ from empathy in one important respect: they focus upon you and your feelings rather than upon the patient and his or her feelings. There is a world of difference between saying 'I sympathize with your distress' and being able to say 'I understand your feelings of turmoil.' Sympathy is easy; anyone can feel sorry for a person in distress. Empathy is trying to feel with, rather than feeling for. It is a very human attribute; while you feel sympathy for an animal in pain, you cannot empathize with it. Empathy means that the helper has understood the feelings that the patient is experiencing. Often this will mean reading between the lines of what the patient is saying, making an informed guess about what the feelings are and sharing this.

Here is a simple example of showing empathy by reading between the lines:

Helper: *'I know that your father and elder sister both had diabetes. I understand that he went blind, and that she had to have a leg amputated before she died last year. Perhaps you're worried about what lies ahead for you?'*

Patient: *I've been told that if I don't smoke or drink, if I keep my blood sugar within the normal range at all times, keep my blood pressure under strict control, make sure that my weight is stable and have regular check-ups, I can reduce the risk of developing complications.'*

Helper: *That sounds like 'yes' to me — you do seem to be worried.*

The avoidance of a direct answer and the recital of the long list of do's and don'ts alerts the helper to the probability that the patient has no real faith or confidence in what he is saying. The helper, therefore, responds to this. When you do this and if your guess (hypothesis sounds better, but it is still only a tentative suggestion put forward on the basis of your knowledge of the patient so far) is correct, the patient will confirm that it is. If it is not right, you will probably be corrected if you have made it clear that your suggestion was only tentative. Either way, your understanding of the patient will have moved forward.

I made up the previous example, but the next one is genuine. It concerns a 59-year-old woman who had been diagnosed as having Type 2 diabetes about 18 months previously. She was not taking her tablets regularly, and consequently her blood glucose was very high. Below, within the brackets, I have commented upon what is happening at each stage and the methods the helper was using to develop an empathic understanding of what she was feeling:

Patient: *'I'm a prisoner of diabetes. "Take these tablets!" "Follow this diet!" "Do this!" "Don't do that!"'*

Helper: *'It sounds as if you feel regimented and pushed around all the time.'* (Helper makes tentative suggestion.)

Patient: *'Not really. It's the constant need to think ahead and plan all the time that I resent.'* (Patient rejects suggestion and gives more information.)

Helper: *'So, it's not so much the routines themselves, it's the loss of freedom and spontaneity that really gets to you.'* (Helper modifies original suggestion and puts forward another.)

Patient: *'That's right! I used to look forward to my retirement. Now I'm not so sure.'* (Patient confirms suggestion and begins to talk about specific concerns.)

Helper: *It's as if your hopes for the future have all been dashed.* (Helper re-phrases what patient has said.)

Patient: *'The doctor says I should be able to lead a normal life, but that's how it feels to me.'*

During this conversation it emerges that the problem is not so much the regimen, but the sense of loss that the patient feels at having been cheated of a healthy and unrestricted retirement. Once these feelings had been clarified, it was possible to help her to see that her reluctance to take her medication was an attempt to deny to herself the fact that she has diabetes. Notice that the helper was responding to leads given by the patient, who remained in control of the conversation. Notice, too, that it *is* a conversation, an interchange of comments and views rather than the type of short, staccato exchange that characterizes the more traditional form of interview and which leads to a submissive apparent compliance:

Patient: *I'm a prisoner of diabetes. "Take these tablets!" "Follow this diet!" "Do this!" "Don't do that!"'*

Helper: *'These things will all help you.'*
Patient: *'Yes, doctor. Thank you, doctor.'*

Reformulating

Trying to rephrase or to reformulate what the patient has said is an important way of developing an empathic understanding. When doing this, try to:

- look for the basic message;
- restate or summarize the basic message in your own words;
- do this in a tentative rather than an absolute way, as this allows the patient to confirm your understanding or correct it if necessary.

Consider a patient who you would like to start on insulin injections, after a period of limited success with oral medication. In response to your suggestion, he says vehemently: 'I don't want injections. Even if my diabetes is getting worse, I want to stay on the tablets.' What is the best way to respond?

The best way is to communicate the message that you realize that there is emotional feeling present but that, at this stage, you are not quite sure what it is. So, a response that tries to decode the feelings is necessary. You are obviously unable to give an appropriate response until you know that you have identified the message correctly. You might say something like: 'It sounds as if you believe that your diabetes is deteriorating and that makes you feel very frightened.' A response such as this does two important things. It puts into different words, (reformulates), what the patient has just said, but it does not distort or deform it. It also tries to identify the underlying feeling. The attempt at identification is tentative and is said in such a way that allows the patient to confirm your hunch, if correct, or put you on the right track if not.

This is better than reacting to the words alone and correcting the factual error. You could have said: 'The fact that you now need insulin injections does not mean that it is getting worse at all. Where did you get that idea from?' This puts the onus back on the patient, who is left trying to find another way of restating his reluctance to start insulin injections. There is also a risk here that the patient will feel scorned and foolish. He may go on the defensive and speak guardedly for the remainder of the session.

Reformulation is the best method because it:

- communicates that you are trying to understand;
- tests your understanding;

- helps patients clarify what they think and feel;
- focuses attention on particular aspects of what was said and encourages the patient to continue.

This reformulation, sometimes called mirroring, or reflecting, is a powerful technique for identifying feelings and helping the patient say more. It can be done in a clumsy way and can be very obvious. It is sometimes caricatured for being mechanistic and artificial. As with all new skills, you may feel that you sound stilted and forced at first. With practice, you will learn to feel comfortable and to sound natural. Egan (1986) suggests that, to respond empathically, you should ask yourself what is the core message being expressed by the patient? Once you feel that you have tentatively identified the core message, you can then check that understanding with the patient. Phrases such as: 'It sounds like . . .'; 'It's as if . . .'; 'It seems that . . .' are helpful in checking your tentative understanding with the patient. This is better than rather bald abrupt openings such as: 'You feel . . .', 'You are . . .' which can sound like dogmatic assertions. If you cannot make sense of what the patient appears to be saying or feeling and you feel confused, ask for clarification. Obviously, you cannot help effectively if you are not sure what is happening.

Remember that the message may appear confusing because the patient is unclear or confused. By asking for clarification, you can often help the patient's own understanding: 'I'm afraid that sounded a bit confusing. Perhaps it was me, or perhaps you feel a bit mixed up about it yourself?'

A short story. To illustrate the importance of looking beyond the words and of trying to identify the core message, here is a short story. It is taken, with some modifications, from one given by Porritt (1990).

Mrs Nidd has just been diagnosed as having Type 2 diabetes and makes her first visit to the diabetes education centre, where she meets the diabetes educator. She asks the nurse: 'Do I need to have injections?' 'No,' says the nurse, 'exercise, diet and tablets will control your blood sugar.' Mrs Nidd then sees the doctor. 'Do I need to have injections?' she asks. 'No,' says the doctor; 'You'll be fine. with tablets, diet and a bit of exercise.' Mrs Nidd goes to see the dietitian. 'Do I need to have injections?' she asks. 'No,' says the dietitian; 'you'll manage with diet, exercise and pills.' Later, the team meets to discuss progress with Mrs Nidd. They discover that she has asked them all, in turn, exactly the same question. 'Oh dear,' each says; 'I hope she's not going to be difficult. We all answered that question. She's just not listening.' Having read books on whole-person care, however, they then realize that it was they who had not been listening. Next time Mrs Nidd visits the centre and again asks: 'Do I need to have injections?', the nurse educator looks at the whole picture, notices the quaver in the voice, the clasped hands and the tension on the face as well as the words themselves and says, 'You sound pretty worried, Mrs Nidd.' 'Not worried, really,' says Mrs Nidd, 'but I've never had anything wrong before and I don't know what to expect.' 'You'd like to talk about what having diabetes means and perhaps ask me some questions?' says the nurse. 'Yes, I would,' says Mrs. Nidd relaxing visibly, and they proceed to do so. The nurse has empathized and has communicated her understanding.

Reassurance

The aim of reassurance is to improve or restore patients' confidence in themselves and in the treatment. Effective reassurance will also maintain their confidence in you. You can give reassurance in a number of ways. Showing respect and interest conveys that you have confidence in them. This, in itself, is reassuring. Giving information and explanations is reassuring because it is helpful in reducing anxiety and uncertainty. Staying calm and using your verbal and non-verbal skills to display confidence and competence gives patients confidence in your competence.

Reassurance is, therefore, a set of skills and behaviours rather than the use of vague but well-meaning words. People sometimes talk very freely about 'giving reassurance', but mean either trying to cheer patients up, or telling them, with varying degrees of subtlety, to pull themselves together. Inappropriate reassurance is not reassuring. It merely emphasizes that the helper has missed the point. Empty words of reassurance such as, 'I'm sure everything will be all right', mean little and may be used by the helper to avoid dealing with emotional issues by sweeping them away.

Trust, confidence and confidentiality

Patients will tend to trust you because of your position, but you can also encourage openness by the way you behave. All the behaviours I have discussed so far are important in promoting trust and confidence. We must also, of course, learn to trust the patients; to trust them to learn for themselves from their own experiences and to make their own decisions. This letting go requires a conscious effort if we are used to caring for people and doing things for them, but it is necessary if we are to show respect. Get it right and the rewards are clear:

'At the time it seemed a hell of a lot to take in, and our concern was whether we would be able to cope. Of course we coped, but the major factor which I think enabled us to face the problem was an atmosphere of trust, of caring, of consideration which was built up by the team of people with whom we came in contact.'

Confidentiality. This is not just a matter of keeping records secure. Patients are entitled to take that for granted. Patients also accept that you work as part of a team and that information has to be shared within the team if their care is to be co-ordinated properly and delivered effectively. Normally, this presents no problems, but sometimes patients will tell you things that it is clear they do not want to go any further, even within the team. This can present you with a very real dilemma. How should you respond to such sensitive information?

There are always limits to confidentiality. Patients will sometimes ask if they can tell you something on the strict condition that you do not write it down in the case-notes, nor tell anyone else about it. It is most unwise to give that sort of undertaking, because you might be unable to keep it. A discussion about why it is so important, or who or what the patient is trying to protect might be sufficient for a more open discussion to take place: 'I'm sorry, I can't give you that sort of promise, but perhaps you can tell me why you are so concerned about it?' If not, do not get yourself into a position of agreeing to hear something and promising to say nothing because multidisciplinary care then becomes very difficult.

Self-disclosure

Patients will often ask you about yourself, either directly or indirectly. They might make comments such as, 'You're so slim, you can't understand what it's like, trying to lose weight.' Or, 'How would you like it if you needed four injections a day every day of your life?' In these examples, trying to identify the underlying message might be the best response. Something like, 'It sounds as if you feel that your efforts to lose weight are not appreciated'; or, 'I guess you're feeling really frustrated with the endless grind of injections' might start a fruitful discussion. Sometimes, however, you might want to say something about yourself and your own experiences of life, or you might think it quite acceptable to give a direct answer to a direct personal question. When is this helpful?

Self-disclosure can be useful if it helps the patient to appreciate the 'normality' of a particular problem, or to give it a different perspective.

Patients often feel that their experiences are unique – which at one level they are, of course – and it can be very comforting to hear that other people have done, or felt, or thought the same. Self-disclosure is unhelpful if it makes the patient feel a failure or if it is done in a patronizing way, for example, 'We've all felt like that sometimes, dear'. A comment such as, 'I was surprised how easy I found it when I decided to give up smoking. It wasn't nearly as bad as I thought it would be' in an attempt to encourage the patient, may well backfire and make the patient feel weak-willed if they are finding the going particularly rough. It is more helpful to acknowledge the difficulties, but to do so in a positive coping manner: 'I found it hard at times, but when I was tempted to light up I reminded myself of all the reasons why I wanted to stop and that helped me over a difficult patch.' Done in this way, you communicate that difficulties are to be expected but can be overcome.

Perhaps this is an appropriate moment to mention that I have Type 1 diabetes. I developed it when I was in my 20s. I do not mention that I have diabetes to patients routinely, and I can think of no good reason for doing so. I mention it if I think that my experiences will help the patient understand their own. To mention it without good cause would be like saying, 'I have diabetes too, so I know what it's like. I know what you're going through', whereas, of course, I may not: my own experience of diabetes may be quite different and it would be presumptuous of me to assume otherwise.

Self-disclosure can help build trust. Patients will feel more confident about being open when they see that they are dealing with someone who is prepared to be open with them. It is not helpful to talk about your personal problems, or situations that have defeated you. There is an exception to this principle, and that is when you are experiencing something that is difficult to hide. If you are tense and distracted because, for example, one of your family is seriously ill or for a similar reason, then denying the obvious has little to recommend it. However, you need not go into detail and should not dwell on it.

You should be wary of disclosing personal opinions. If you say something like, 'I think you should have a good talk to your husband about his behaviour' this sets you up as an expert in what the patient should do. If the patient acts on your suggestion and it all goes horribly wrong, you then have to stand by your advice and accept responsibility for it and for the consequences. A better way of opening up the topic might be to say something like, 'I imagine that you have weighed up the pros and cons of having a good talk with him?'

Humour

As you read books on counselling, you can easily come away with the impression that when you talk to patients you have to be earnest and sincere at all times and that there is no place for lightheartedness or banter in the helping relationship. This is not true. The ability to laugh at oneself and at one's predicament is a precious asset, and humour can be found even in the most difficult and trying circumstances. Badly timed or ill-judged attempts at humour, of course, can be offensive and destructive, so you need to know the patient well. The key is to laugh *with* the patient, never *at* him or her.

People sometimes use humour because they are embarrassed or ill at ease. Humour is a way of keeping painful topics at bay. It can also be a way of saying something barbed or hurtful in an apparently lighthearted manner. Whenever patients use humour, it is worth trying to understand why. You have the choice then of responding to the joke or to the underlying reason.

Concluding Remarks

In this chapter I have contrasted different ways of helping from, at one extreme, the traditional stance that regards patients as recipients of the helper's wisdom, to, at the other, one that sees patients as equal partners in the care process. It is my belief that the latter more accurately reflects the nature of the relationship for which we should be striving, and that this can be supported on clinical and humanitarian grounds. Of course, this threatens traditional power structures, and can be attacked as being both fashionable and impractical. In the short-term it undoubtedly does take extra time, and I am well aware that this is always in short supply in a ward, consulting room or surgery. On the other hand, if the extra time that is spent is recouped in terms of better satisfied and more independent patients with a reduced frequency of diabetes-related disorders, is the time not well spent? I cannot prove this because the evidence is incomplete, but what evidence exists is highly suggestive.

I have spent much of this chapter in trying to show that empowerment is not just an abstract philosophical concept or an impractical ideal but something that can be achieved by holding certain attitudes and possessing certain skills. The interpersonal relationship between helper and patient is the vehicle in which all care is delivered: I have tried to show how conditions of genuineness, respect and empathy can be generated and used to facilitate whole-person care.

Summary

❏ The helping relationship is the foundation of all care. The most appropriate relationship to strive for is one in which the patient is empowered.

❏ To empower patients means to value and promote their active participation in management. It requires that helpers show respect, acceptance and trust. It requires that helpers behave in ways that promote autonomy and that give patients skills, information and support.

❏ These aims and values can be implemented by taking care over what you do, how you do it and where you do it.

❏ The physical setting where you work should afford privacy, comfort and minimal status barriers.

❏ Key helper qualities include genuineness, respect, empathy, and reassurance. These promote trust and confidence.

❏ Genuineness can be achieved by being yourself rather than an anonymous professional, and by being honest and consistent.

❏ Respect is shown by actions that protect a patient's dignity and privacy; listening to what patients are saying; trying to help them mobilize their own resources; explaining procedures and actions before carrying them out, and by giving choices wherever possible.

❏ Empathy is shown by listening to what the patient is saying and by penetrating beyond the words. You can do this by looking for the basic message; restating or summarizing the basic message in your own words and doing this in a tentative rather than an absolute way.

❏ Reassurance involves showing respect and interest; giving information and explanations and behaving in a confident coping manner.

❏ It is often helpful to tell patients things about yourself, or to use humour, because they can help patients appreciate the normality of a particular problem or give it a different perspective. These things must be done in a way that avoids making the patient feel foolish or inferior.

5

Understanding and Exploring: the Skills of Good Communication

In this chapter I shall focus upon using communication skills as the basis for exploring, understanding and acting. To communicate effectively we must be able to say what we mean. We must listen accurately so that we hear and understand what patients are saying. We must also make sure that patients know that we have heard and understood. In addition, we need to be able to respond appropriately to both the words and to the feelings that lie behind them.

Good Communication Skills Have To Be Learned

Are you are a brilliant conversationalist? On a train journey, can you strike up scintillating discussions with total strangers? As a public speaker do you hold an audience spellbound with your wit and wisdom? If so, does this mean that you will be any good at communicating with your patients? No, it does not. You might be quite useless. Communication in health care requires specialized expertise and the skills all have to be learned:

'I went to see my doctor with pins and needles and a patch of numbness in my left leg. He sent me to see the neurologist at the local hospital. I arrived in good time, followed the signposts without difficulty, was greeted politely by the receptionist and settled down to wait. The waiting area was nicely furnished and decorated. There were no delays and at the appointment time I was collected by a nurse and taken to the consulting-room. So far so good. As the nurse held the door open for me, I could see the doctor (at least, I assume he was a doctor, he never did introduce himself) sitting behind a desk. Without looking up, he began asking questions. In the time it took me to walk from the door to the chair in front of the desk he had established my handedness (left) and my age (41). I never quite recovered from the surprise of this abrupt beginning and remember nothing else from the session. Actually, this is a slight exaggeration. I

remember that I handed him a list of my symptoms that I had written earlier in case I forgot; he took it and put it in the case-notes without looking at it.'

This patient is describing a highly skilled performance. If you doubt this, then I suggest that you take the next new patient who comes to see you and establish their age and 'handedness' while they are still framed in your doorway. You will find it extremely difficult to suspend the rules of normal social conduct in the way the neurologist did. So, in one sense, it was a highly skilled performance. Unfortunately, the skills were entirely destructive.

Encounters with health workers are very different to other interpersonal encounters and it is easy to get away with behaviour that would be unacceptably bizarre in other contexts. We must prevent this from happening because communication serves a number of important purposes, for example it:

- helps to form and develop the relationship;
- facilitates psychological support;
- identifies problems accurately;
- is necessary for explanations and education;
- reduces inappropriate or unnecessary investigations;
- promotes self-care;
- enables the helper to monitor progress;
- increases patient satisfaction.

In other words, the quality of communication is central to the whole process of care, and your skills will play a large part in determining patients' adaptation and actions. When communication is poor, all of this is put in jeopardy. It is easy to give examples, but two will be enough to make the point:

- A patient with Type 2 diabetes was discharged from a hospital clinic back to her doctor. She believed that she was being discharged because she had been cured.
- A patient was most indignant when she was told that she had problems with her nerves. She thought this meant that she was 'mental'. In fact, she was developing neurological complications.

It is essential, therefore, that the messages that patients receive are those that we want them to receive. Correspondingly, it is just as important that we understand what patients are saying to us. Communication can be broken down into a number of components, which I will now explore.

Non-Verbal Communication

By non-verbal communication I mean communication between the participants without using words. Sometimes this is done intentionally (a quizzical frown; raised eyebrows expressing surprise), and sometimes it is done unintentionally (a half-stifled yawn; a glance at the clock). If you ask patients how a session went, they will often comment upon how the helper behaved, rather than upon what was actually said: 'He seemed very rushed'; or 'She seemed very concerned.' This illustrates the importance of the non-verbal aspects of communication: what you say is only part of the message. The way in which you deliver your words and your body language are just as important. Get it right and patients will leave at the end of a session feeling that you have understood them. They will be more satisfied with the session and more likely to act on any actions you have agreed. Get it wrong and it will not just be time that was wasted; confidence in you will have been dented and you may have to struggle to get it back.

The main components of non-verbal communication are as follows:

Body posture. When seated, aim at what is sometimes described as an 'open' body posture. This means sitting at a slight angle to the other person. This avoids squaring up to each other, which can seem threatening. Sitting at an angle means that you can look at each other, or glance away, with equal comfort. Leaning slightly forward communicates interest and alertness. You might think that if you lean back in your chair in a casual manner this will indicate that you are relaxed and unhurried, but to many patients it will suggest boredom and disinterest. Folding your arms or legs may communicate defensiveness, and is best avoided.

Movement and gesture. A smile communicates warmth, a fixed grin insincerity. Aim to avoid flamboyant or expansive gestures as these are distracting. Try not to fidget as this tends to signal impatience or lack of interest. Nods are useful and encourage a person to continue talking, but beware of overdoing it. This can be a danger when you are trying to encourage a quiet patient to be more open.

Eye contact. This allows each participant to see that they are being listened to and to gauge what effect each is having on the other. People vary in the extent to which they use eye contact, so you will have to adjust your own to match that of the patient. Aim at steady eye contact while in conversation, but do not stare. If your gaze is very intense, patients will feel uncomfortable. On the other hand, if you avoid eye contact, patients may think that you are concealing something. Avoid looking away for long periods. The view out of the window might be very interesting, but your job is to concentrate upon the patient's world, not the world at large.

Proximity. Aim at a distance between you that feels comfortable; neither too far apart nor too close together.

Paralinguistic cues. This piece of jargon refers to how people speak; such as the speed, fluency and volume of speech. You can learn more about patients from paying attention to these things. Notice that a shy patient is likely to be soft-spoken and hesitant, whereas one who is angry or insistent will speak loudly and give you little opportunity to squeeze in your replies before interrupting. For yourself, you should try to avoid extremes, but be prepared to be flexible where necessary. For example, you will need to speak more slowly and clearly if a patient has problems in hearing or understanding.

These are guidelines rather than rules. Spoken language has formal rules of grammar and syntax, but although we talk of body language, there are no firm rules for non-verbal communication. This is because it is influenced by a variety of other factors. Take proximity, for instance; the distance between patient and helper at which each feels comfortable is affected by the cultural background of the participants.

Age is also a factor. We feel comfortable being close to children and it is often quite natural to touch them. However, touch means quite different things to adults who may feel patronized, embarrassed, or sexually threatened. Some professionals, of course, such as nurses or chiropodists, require physical contact as an essential part of their daily activities, but others such as dietitians or psychologists do not and they may feel it to be inappropriate to touch adult patients at all, apart from a handshake. It can be difficult to manage even a reassuring pat on the arm for fear of how it will be interpreted.

Practising non-verbal communication

The helper who is inexperienced, unskilled, or ill-at-ease, will tend to give inconsistent or contradictory messages and may misunderstand the behaviour of the patient or react inappropriately to it. A skilled helper can integrate all aspects of non-verbal communication with the words themselves to produce a coherent message in which the emotional tone is appropriate.

Try to monitor your own vocal and non-verbal behaviour when you are with patients. Notice how they change according to who you are with, where you are and how you are feeling. Notice how some patients will make you feel impatient or slightly irritated. Others will make you feel eager to do all you can to help. How does this show in your behaviour? What do reactions such as these tell you about the patient, and what, just as importantly, do they say about you?

At the same time, try to attend to the body language of the patient. This will help you to understand their internal state and how your messages are being received. If you have not thought about this before, it can be helpful to spend some time observing how people who are deep in conversation with each other behave in normal social situations; how they stand or sit, or how they emphasize a particular message by means of hand gestures. Can you describe how people show reactions such as agreement or puzzlement? Notice how the body language is used to reinforce a verbal message and how it is generally consistent with a person's internal state. When somebody is depressed, for example, the body movements become slower and smaller, the voice becomes flat, the eyes become downcast. How do people reveal other moods, such as anxiety or apprehension (often unwittingly) through their body language? Look for inconsistencies. If a patient says that they feel relaxed but you notice a foot tapping, the jaw clenching and the neck and face flushing, what would you conclude?

Verbal Communication

'My son, my child! From humble lips may fall wise words, methinks.'
                    (Sophocles, translated by Gilbert Murray)

'See here son, this slave talks sense.'
                    (Sophocles, translated by Ezra Pound)

These are two different versions of the same line from a play by Sophocles. As I do not know Classical Greek, I am unable to say which is the more accurate translation, but I can say that the second is the easier to understand and so has the greater impact. I can hardly expect that too many translators will be struggling with my words in 2000 years' time, but I am certain that the words we use can help communication, or they can hinder it. What sort of language should we use with our patients? How can we use words to say what we mean? How can words reflect feelings? Since most of our encounters start with a question, even if it is only 'Good morning. Are you Mrs. Smith?', I shall start by looking at some of the issues concerned with the use of questions.

Asking questions

Questions are asked for many reasons: to gather information about what a patient thinks, feels, knows or does; to identify problems and strengths; to encourage conversation, to make a request and so forth. There are different sorts of questions, some of which are useful on particular occasions and some which are best avoided at all times.

Open questions. As the name indicates, open questions have no right or desirable answer and have no point of view underlying them. Questions such as: 'How do you feel when . . .?' 'What happened after . . .?' 'What are you worried about at the moment . . .?' are typical open questions. They are particularly useful at helping to get to know a patient better, at helping patients to open up and say more and talking about opinions and feelings. This is because they encourage full, informative answers.

Closed questions. Closed questions are ones that require a short answer, often a simple yes or no, or a simple piece of information: 'What dose of Tolbutemide are you on?'; 'Have you seen the dietitian yet?' They are useful for discovering facts, but they limit the possibilities of a true dialogue developing. Too many closed questions produce a very stilted, unnatural, conversation and can make patients feel that they are being interrogated. In addition, the answers you get may not always be those you want to hear because closed questions can appear challenging:

Irritable ophthalmologist, trying to test the intraocular pressure of a patient who keeps blinking at the critical moment: *'I've been doing this test for years and haven't had a failure yet. Are you going to be the first?'*

Irritated patient, refusing to be cowed: *'Yes.'*

Leading questions. These are questions containing an assumption that is very difficult to argue against, for example, 'There's no need to be afraid of injections, is there?' This assumes that the patient is afraid of injections. Leading questions are extremely difficult to answer as there is no simple response. Under normal circumstances, try not to ask questions that make assumptions. It takes great confidence on the part of the patient to disagree with you. Having said that, there are some occasions when leading questions can be very useful and I will mention them later.

Multiple questions. It is easy to ask questions that contain several parts to them. The problem here is that it is difficult to understand the response because it is unclear which part of the question the patient is responding to:

Helper: *'Do you think that the difficulties in keeping to the diet are mostly because you cook for all the family, or mostly because you have a sweet-tooth?'*

Patient: *'Yes.'*

Helper: *'Sorry! Did you mean 'yes' to the fact that you do all the cooking, or 'yes' to having a sweet-tooth?'*

Patient: *'Yes.'*

Keep your questions simple. Ask them one at a time.

Questions with a moral tone. Some questions have an air of censure about them: 'Do you feel guilty about not testing your blood sugar as often as you should?' This is also a leading question. If you want your patients to clam-up and feel uncomfortable, this is the style to use. Otherwise, avoid questions that imply judgements about the patient.

You can often help patients to give open responses by making a general remark before asking a specific question. For example, if you want to ask about blood glucose testing and you do not want the patient to tell you what they think you want to hear, you could say, 'People often have difficulty in testing their blood sugar as often as they would like, for one reason or another. I'd like to talk about any problems you have experienced, so we can try and sort them out.' Then ask about frequency of testing. This transmits the message that having difficulties is respectable and not something to conceal. You can also use an opening statement when helping patients talk about their emotions and feelings: 'Many patients are surprised about how angry they feel about having diabetes; perhaps you've felt this way?'

'Why?' questions. Everyone wants to know why things are the way they are, but these questions are of limited value. When patients ask you why certain things happen, you may find it extremely difficult to give an adequate answer: 'Why has my son developed diabetes?'; 'Why do I have to do all these blood tests?' There may be no simple answer you can give to questions like the first, and a question like the second seems to be more a cry of frustration than a request for information. You can imagine, therefore, how patients feel when you unleash 'why' questions on them: 'Why do you find it so hard to keep to the diet?' There is no simple answer, and the question sounds like an accusation.

It is better to ask questions that aim to uncover the circumstances under which controlled eating is difficult, the feelings that accompany it, and the eating behaviour itself: 'When is it hardest to keep to the diet?'; 'When is it easy to keep to the diet?'; 'How does your mood effect what you eat?'; 'When you find it hard to keep to the diet, what sorts of food do you go for?'

Although I have just given several examples in a row, try to avoid launching a fusillade of questions all at once. As I explained earlier, this can appear intimidatory.

'Why' questions also imply an intellectual frame of reference. This will be inappropriate if you are trying to understand a patient's feelings. Imagine that you are with a patient who has a very woebegone expression. Which of these alternatives is likely to be the more helpful?:

- 'I'm sorry to see you look upset. Can you tell me how you feel at the moment?'
- 'I'm sorry to see you look upset. Why are you upset?'

The first is the better alternative because the second requires explanation and analysis. It does not deal with the feeling itself.

Questions that supply the answer. It is easy to prompt patients by supplying the answer we expect. This is common if a patient is very quiet or unresponsive, such as a teenager giving you the silent treatment: 'I noticed that you pulled a face when I mentioned your stepmother. Was that because you don't like her?' It is also common if mutual understanding is limited by language difficulties. If you were abroad, you might cope by simply speaking louder, but in clinic the usual technique is to provide the answer yourself: 'Why are things at home so tense? Is it because you think your parents are old-fashioned and too strict?' This also occurs if we are not very self-confident and when we are observed, such as when another member of the team or a trainee is present. Try not to prompt the patient in this manner because you cannot rely on the answers you receive. Paradoxically, you are more likely to believe them because they are ones that you have supplied.

Questions that are not questions. Sometimes our questions are not really questions at all. 'Good morning. How are you today?' is more of a social ritual than a question, a preliminary (and an important one) to the core business of the session. Sometimes, though, we ask questions because we are stuck, or at a loss about what to do next, so a question can be a way of buying time in the hope that you think of something, or on the off-chance that something interesting will emerge. Such questions may serve their purpose, but a better solution is to have a proper structure to your session. I will have more to say about this later.

Sometimes we make statements but disguise them as questions by our tone of voice: 'What are we going to do with you?' When this is said to a patient with consistently high blood glucose, it may sound light-hearted and this may be the spirit in which it is intended, but it may also signal exasperation. It can sound rather like the kind of non-question that a parent who has waited up until the small hours might ask their errant child ('What time do you call this, then?'), so when we do it to patients it is hardly surprising if they begin to feel like a guilty child again, even when they have done nothing wrong.

You will have noticed from the examples that many of the styles of questions are not mutually exclusive, so it is possible to cram many errors into just one question. You will also have noticed that different styles serve different purposes. Simple or precise information is best acquired with closed questions, while open questions encourage conversations and self-disclosure. The purpose underlying your questions will help to determine how they should be phrased. Keep questions simple at all times. This applies to the language you use and to the sentence structure. Anything that causes confusion, which is ambiguous or leads the patient in a certain direction should be avoided.

One question that should become well polished through frequent usage is 'What questions would you like to ask me?' This is a leading question, and I defend it on the grounds that by making the assumption that patients have questions, they will come to accept that asking questions is positively encouraged. If patients are not used to being involved in the sessions, this question will catch them unprepared and they may only think of important questions on the journey home. It may be helpful to suggest that they write them down and bring them along next time.

Responding to questions. Patients will often ask you questions. Questions are used not just to request information, but to express doubt, worries or to transmit other messages. In the short story I quoted in an earlier chapter, Mrs Nidd's repeated question: 'Do I need to have injections?' reflected her anxieties about her ill-health and the future. The factual reply she kept being given was not effective because it did not acknowledge or address the underlying worries. If you are not sure why a question has been asked, and you think that giving the obvious or straightforward answer will simply close the topic without really understanding why it was raised, you can always say 'It would help me to know why you ask that, before I try and answer it.' This is probably better than simply asking: 'Why do you ask that?', as some patients will think that you are avoiding answering by parrying one question with another.

Sometimes patients ask questions at an inconvenient time in the session for you to give a proper answer; perhaps you need more information, perhaps you need the result of a blood test or some other investigation. The best plan is to acknowledge the question and say that you will answer it as soon as you are able: 'I'll do my best to remember to answer that when I am able to do so, but if you think that I have forgotten, please remind me.'

Active Listening

'I don't think that people at the clinic like listening to me. They seem to be much happier when they are doing all the talking.'

One of the most important skills that you will need, and one that will determine the extent to which you are able to acquire and demonstrate an accurate understanding of patients, is the skill of active listening. Listening is often devalued because it is not seen as being very skilled or very productive. The exact reverse is true. Listening is hard work, far removed from just sitting there and saying nothing. For these reasons, it is often referred to as active listening.

Active listening is made up of many of the individual skills that I have already covered. I shall outline them again for the sake of clarity:

• Non-verbal communication, by
  – eye contact – look at patients when they talk;
  – open posture – to indicate that you are interested.

- Verbal behaviour, by
  - responding to the patient by reflecting;
  - using comments such as 'I see what you mean' or 'I follow you' which signal that you are listening and which encourage the patient to continue;
  - avoiding sending discouraging messages by interrupting, changing the subject, not acknowledging what the patient says and interrogative questioning.
- Concentrating upon the patient, by
  - trying to understand what the patient is saying and feeling, so that you can respond appropriately.

Barriers to active listening

Even when we try to give the patient our whole attention and concentration, we remain vulnerable to a wide range of biases and distractions that can easily get in the way. I shall list some of the most common and suggest ways of overcoming them.

Distractions. There is never any shortage of things to distract you from giving your full attention to the patient. You may be concerned with your own inner feelings and preoccupations. You might want to hurry things along, aware that the clinic is running late and that patients have to get back to work, or have to pick up children from school. Perhaps today, of all days, you wanted to get off early yourself as you have to take the cat to the vet. Or, it may be that what the patient has just said has triggered off a train of thought of your own. Perhaps you are busy thinking about how to respond to something the patient just said that struck you as being particularly important, and you are only half-listening to what is being said right now.

Feeling responsible. Helpers sometimes put themselves under pressure by thinking that every problem has to have a solution and that they personally have to know what the solution is and be able to implement it. Sometimes patients have to live in such appalling circumstances or with such terrible problems that you want desperately to help. Wanting to help people is, after all, why most of us trained to do the job we do. These are particular dangers for recently qualified helpers who feel that they have to prove themselves to themselves, to the patient and to their colleagues in order to win their therapeutic spurs as soon as possible. This self-imposed pressure makes active listening difficult because it means that you are always concentrating on yourself and trying to think of things to do or say rather than concentrating upon what the patient is doing or saying.

Culture gaps. It is hard to listen successfully to people whose background and culture are far removed from your own, because they may be describing things that are quite different from your own experiences and expectations. You may have stereotypes about people with a particular background that make it difficult to listen objectively. You may filter out things the patient says that do not conform to your preconceptions.

Feeling uncomfortable. If you feel more at home exploring the physical world of your patients rather than the emotional one, you may focus on that to the exclusion of everything else:

Patient: *'I'm worried about my eyesight. I'm frightened of the laser treatment; I don't think it's going to work. I keep thinking that I must have brought it on myself by not looking after my blood sugar over all those years.'* (sobs)

Helper: *'Er, what was your blood sugar this morning?'*

Referring to the case-notes. If you spend a lot of time reading the case file, or making notes, you will miss a lot of information through not observing or listening to the patient.

Interrupting. Inexperienced or unconfident helpers may feel that they have to do most of the talking. They may decide very quickly what they want to hear from the patient and frequently interrupt to keep control over the session. If you interrupt the patient you give a clear message that you are not really interested in what they are saying. Avoid butting-in if possible.

Categorization. Helpers may try to shoehorn patients into compartments. This is tempting because once we can label a patient, we are on familiar territory and can proceed on automatic pilot without having to think too much. 'Difficult personality' or 'unmotivated' are just two of the labels that you might recognize as being ones that we sometimes use to justify our actions.

Another form of categorization occurs when we find that, thanks to certain priorities of our own, what the patient 'needs' turns out to be exactly what we have to offer:

You are sitting in the office, having just taken delivery of some new reflectance meters. These are an improved model that is capable of greater accuracy than the old version although they are rather harder to operate. Older patients find the control buttons small and fiddly and have trouble reading the display. On the other hand, they can store several months' worth of results and can perform a range of statistical analyses on the readings. With a simple interconnecting cable (free from the sales rep.) the stored data can be downloaded to your personal computer where frequency of self-monitoring is automatically plotted against blood glucose control. Just the thing for your on-going project into the relationship between frequency of self-monitoring and blood glucose levels.

What are the odds of discovering that the next patient through the door will be in crying need of just this machine, despite arthritic fingers and failing eyesight?

Overcoming barriers to active listening

To minimize the risk of these distortions happening, we need to monitor ourselves and to be aware of the influences and biases that get in the way of hearing patients properly. Egan (1986) points out that skilled helpers periodically monitor their own verbal and non-verbal behaviour during a session for hints of bias, self-preoccupation and distractions. To do this, he suggests that we regularly ask ourselves a number of questions. His list includes:

- Am I aware of my biases and my ability to listen?
- Do I listen to what is going on inside myself as I interact with the client?
- What distracts me from listening more carefully, and what can I do to manage these distractions?
- Am I reading the patient's non-verbal behaviours and seeing how they modify what he or she is saying verbally?

Going through the list of barriers will also suggest specific solutions. For example, if you have to make notes or refresh your memory from the notes, you can always ask the patient to wait for a moment. This is more respectful than ignoring the patient, or trying to read and write and concentrate on listening at the same time. Similarly, if a patient is very talkative and you feel you have to get back on course, you could say something like 'I'm sorry to interrupt, but ...' or: 'Perhaps we could return to that later ...'

Exploring Feelings

If you focus on physical symptoms alone and then give advice or recommend some action, there is a strong chance that the patient will not be receptive to what you have to say. This is because you have not explored the patient's psychological world, and he or she may be too preoccupied with undisclosed thoughts and feelings to concentrate upon what you are saying. The presence of strong emotions that are not identified or acknowledged will prevent open communication from taking place. It is only when you have understood the patient's emotions and concerns that you can move on to explore the best way to help. You cannot do that properly when you can only see half the picture.

The skills I have discussed so far are all important in the exploration of feelings. In the following fictitious example, I have inserted comments in the brackets at each stage about what the helper is trying to achieve and what skills are being used.

Patient: *'I've been very worried about my eyes recently.'*

Helper: *'Would you like to tell me about it, please?'* (Helper uses an open question to encourage the patient to continue; does not focus on either symptoms or feelings at this stage, but waits for the patient to take the initiative.)

Patient: *'Sometimes my vision seems very sharp and at other times it goes sort of blurred.'*

Helper: *'I see. So it varies quite a lot?'* (Helper begins to clarify. Since the patient has chosen to talk about symptoms, they focus on that first.)

[Later, the helper brings the conversation back to the patient's initial expression of worry.]

Helper: *'You said earlier that you were worried about your eyes. What worries you in particular?'* (Helper acknowledges emotion and seeks clarification.)

Patient: *'I'm worried I might be losing my sight. If that happened I don't know how my wife and I would cope.'*

Helper: *'I can see that must be a big worry for you. Can you tell me why you think you are losing your sight?'* (Helper acknowledges emotion and asks for clarification using an open question.)

Patient: *'Well, my father had diabetes and he went blind.'*

Helper: *'Mm. Do you have clear memories of that?'* (Clarification.)

Patient: *'Yes. He became very depressed and I remember that my mother had a terrible time with him.'* (sighs)

Helper: *'I guess that you are afraid of the same thing happening to you.'* (Empathic reformulation.)

Notice that questions are balanced by statements. The helper does not dominate the conversation but engages in a true dialogue.

Barriers to exploring feelings

Fear of losing control. Helpers sometimes have a fear of becoming over-burdened with patients' problems, of making mistakes, of becoming involved, or of opening the floodgates to emotional outpourings that will overwhelm them. They develop a protective shell to shield them from becoming upset, and develop ways of distancing themselves from having to deal with feelings (*'I'm just a nurse; you'll have to ask the doctor about that.'*). These methods prevent you from recognizing or acknowledging feelings in others.

Feeling anxious. Dealing with strong feelings in others can arouse strong feelings in ourselves. When people are embarrassed or ill-at-ease they often talk too much. You may also find that you speak more quickly than usual, and that your questions or explanations become longer and more complicated. Your awareness of time may alter when you are anxious, so you may also find that you attempt to fill any apparent pauses or silences in the conversation before they last an eternity. You become more concerned with monitoring your own internal state than with attending to the patient. Such changes in our behaviour are spotted by the patient, who reacts to them, perhaps by becoming more ill-at-ease and a vicious circle is formed.

Overcoming the barriers to exploring feelings

Even the most experienced and confident helpers find themselves ill-at-ease in certain situations, but they have learned to recognize the situations or the symptoms in themselves and have learned to cope with them. You can:

* Identify what you find difficult by introspection and monitoring yourself during your sessions with patients. If you become hesitant, tongue-tied or feel ill-at-ease when discussing a particular topic, or try to avoid it altogether, these are good signs that you have identified a problem area.
* Identify in what ways your behaviour changes. Again, introspection is useful, or if you do joint interviews, you could ask a colleague for feedback.

Coping with extremes of emotion

You can expect to see patients in a state of strong emotion. Sometimes this will be related to having diabetes, and sometimes it will be because strong emotions are a part of life. Degrees of anger, anxiety and depression are not uncommon. Patients (and parents, too) may feel angry with you for some reason, or the anger may be directed towards themselves but be expressed at you. High levels of anger are usually a reaction to diagnosis, to a significant change in day-to-day coping ability, or may reflect the frustration a patient feels about their predicament and fears for the future. Feelings of anxiety and depression may also be a response to thoughts of the future, or reactions to a period of poor control, despite their best efforts.

In all these situations, your relationship-building and communication skills will be important. Maintaining an accepting manner will transmit the message that you are not rejecting the patient or their feelings. Many helpers find anger particularly difficult to deal with because it is hard not to feel personally under attack. You should try to stay calm, at least on the outside. This means not becoming agitated in your movements, while continuing to speak at your usual pace and volume, if not slightly slower. Do not argue. It is usually best to acknowledge that the patient is angry, and gently enquire why. This generally takes the heat out of the situation, but may leave you feeling drained. If you have calmed an agitated patient, or stemmed the tears of one who is deeply upset, you may feel the need to talk about your own feelings to a colleague. There is more about this in Chapter 8.

Structuring a Session

Have you ever tried to catch a bus in a strange town in a foreign country and you don't understand the language? Everybody rushes along, seeming to know exactly what to do and where to go – except you. You feel disorientated and intimidated. Many people experience this when they visit a hospital or clinic. They feel psychologically jostled. To you, with your familiarity with the situation, there is no problem. You feel relaxed and in control. To patients, however, this is alien territory, both psychologically and physically, and they are not quite sure how to behave. This extends into the session, where it often takes some time to settle down and feel in tune with what is happening. By then it may be too late, and the session is nearly over. You may have felt a little of this unease yourself if you make the very occasional home visit; now you are on the patient's territory and the rules that govern the meeting no longer seem so clear. Should you be on your best professional behaviour, or can you relax a bit and make it something of a social visit as well? No matter where you hold your sessions you should try to make sure that your meetings have a clear purpose and structure. The hardest parts are starting a session and knowing how to end it.

Starting a session

Introductions. First impressions are very important. When possible, collect the patient personally rather than have him or her ushered in to your presence. Greet the patient with a smile and, where appropriate, a handshake. If you have not met before, speak your name clearly and mention your job or title. Establish how each patient would like to be addressed. This is particularly important at either end of the age range. Youngsters reach an age when they feel patronized if you call them by their first name. Older people feel this too, and often find such familiarity intrusive.

Give the patient time to settle down. A minute or so spent in non-clinical conversation is very helpful in allowing patients who feel anxious to relax a little. It can also give patients a greater sense of satisfaction with the session, because they are more likely to feel you are treating them as real human beings rather than as malfunctioning organisms.

Can you identify the patient's feelings? If you are seeing the patient for the first time and you observe that he or she looks anxious or concerned, it is a good idea to mention this by saying something like 'I expect you feel rather anxious, being here for the first time', and pause for a reply. This transmits several important messages: first, that you expect patients to have feelings; second, that you have noticed them and third, that it is quite in order to talk about them. If you know the patient better, be alert for evidence that there is something on the patient's mind: fidgeting, downcast expression or sighing are obvious signs. A comment such as 'You look thoroughly out of sorts today' signals your interest in their emotional state.

Clarify why you are both there. The next task is to clarify the purpose of the session you are about to have. This is not always obvious to the patient. It may not be obvious to you either, unless you have a clear action plan to guide you. Such confusion is a particular risk if your appointments are organized around the needs of the calendar rather than around the needs of the patient. Ask yourself: *'What do I hope to achieve from this session?'* You both need to be clear about why you are meeting.

How much time is available? Patients are used to short appointments and gear themselves up accordingly. If you plan to spend a reasonable length of time or longer than normal with the patient, mentioning the time available will help them relax and pace themselves through the session. Their concentration will suffer if they spend the session in fear of missing the bus.

The middle of a session

Erect signposts. If you are covering much ground, perhaps trying to get an overview of a patient you are meeting for the first time, all the patient may experience is a disjointed or confusing series of questions. It is very helpful, therefore, to give a clear signal when you are about to start a new tack. Something like 'I'd like to spend some time now discussing how you and your wife cope with diabetes' or, 'Let's move on to talk about how exercise can fit in with your lifestyle' would be appropriate.

Ending a session

Wind up. If you simply close the session without a warning or a winding up phase, you will be seen as brusque. It is often said that patients reveal important fears or ask important questions towards the end of a session, so start to wind up a few minutes before the end, and tell the patient the session is nearly over. If he or she does mention something that is clearly important and you have no time to deal with it adequately, do not attempt to tackle it there and then because you will find yourself rushed. Instead, give a clear indication that you have heard and make an undertaking to discuss it properly next meeting.

Summarize. Summaries are useful and serve a number of purposes. A summary makes a natural ending, reminding the participants of the key points of the session, clarifying what was achieved and what has to be done. If you have agreed some management goals during the session or made some other commitments, now is the time to remind yourselves of what they were. If you have been giving some information, briefly recap the main points. Because the summary is important, leave time for it.

Concluding Remarks

Unless you can communicate effectively, your ability to help patients will be severely curtailed because good communication underpins almost everything that you do. In this chapter I have tried to identify the main components of good communication, and to give examples of its practical importance in diabetes care.

Sometimes the ability to communicate is described as a gift that you may or may not possess. It is not. It is a set of skills that can be identified and practised. People may tell you that this is a very mechanistic approach and that the ability to communicate is more an art than a science. This, too, is wrong. I shall end this chapter by making two observations. First, one of the main complaints that patients level against staff is that they are very poor at communication and that they, the patients, feel excluded from their own care because of it. Second, when groups of staff have been taught communication skills, the level of satisfaction reported by patients rises significantly, and staff themselves report higher levels of job satisfaction. All helpers can and should attempt to improve their communication skills.

Summary

☐ Good communication serves a number of important purposes. It is necessary for understanding, explanations and education. It facilitates the giving of psychological support and increases patients' satisfaction with the session.

☐ The skills of good communication can be learned.

☐ The main components of non-verbal communication are posture, movement and gesture, eye contact and proximity.

☐ Pay attention to the speed and volume of your speech.

☐ When asking questions use open questions where possible because they have no right answers and because they encourage a patient to give full, informative answers.

☐ Types of question that are best avoided, or have limited value, include leading questions, those with a moral tone and those that ask why.

☐ Listening is hard work. The skills of active listening include attending to your own non-verbal communication and verbal behaviour and those of the patient.

☐ There are many potential barriers to active listening. Try to identify biases and distractions when they occur.

☐ It is important to identify and acknowledge patients' emotions and feelings. The skills of empathy and open listening are helpful.

☐ When meeting a patient for the first time, introduce yourself and establish how the patient would like to be addressed.

☐ Sessions benefit from having a clear structure. Help the patient to settle down if necessary by a few moments of non-clinical conversation. Be alert for clues to the patient's emotional state and comment on it if appropriate.

☐ When faced with extremes of emotions, use your communication skills to establish why the patient is so aroused. If the patient is angry, do not argue. Behave in a calm, controlled manner, even if you are quaking inside.

☐ Towards the end of a session, begin to wind up a few minutes beforehand. Summarize the main contents of the session, the main conclusions reached and any tasks that either of you need to perform before the next appointment.

6

Counselling in Life Change and Life Crisis

'Sometimes I just have to resign myself to living with diabetes. Sometimes diabetes just has to resign itself to living with me.'

Adaptation to diabetes is not something that happens once and can then be forgotten. If you have diabetes, everything you do colours the disease and the disease colours everything you do. This chapter is about helping and supporting patients through a lifetime of diabetes and, specifically, through periods of stress, change and crisis.

If you were to list some of the important personal events that you might experience during your life, your list would probably contain many of the following: as a youngster, changing school, examinations, leaving home and starting work; as a young adult, marriage, parenthood or changing a job; and, as an older person, family bereavements and retirement. The list could be extended almost endlessly. You will sometimes see such events as these described as major life events, or as psychosocial transitions or life crises. They may, of course, provide opportunities for development and personal growth, but they may also involve a period of stress and disruption. When they occur, they are often associated with periods of disturbed psychological adjustment. When they occur to someone who has diabetes, they may also be associated with periods of altered adjustment to the disease.

One change that all patients experience is that of learning that they have developed diabetes. I will start, therefore, by giving some guidance on how to break the news and how to help the patient make the transition from being well to being chronically ill.

The Crisis of Diagnosis: Breaking Bad News

Not all professionals have the responsibility of telling patients that they have developed diabetes. Most, however, have contact with patients in the weeks following diagnosis, at a time when they might feel overwhelmed, have forgotten much of what they have been told, and may be bewildered and confused. It is not sufficient just to give the diagnosis and leave it at that; you need to know how to support the patient afterwards. You have to help the patient begin to plan for the future in a positive way and begin to learn self-management skills. You must also know how to help patients deal with other forms of bad news, such as the development of degenerative complications or difficulties associated with pregnancy, and the same skills are relevant in these situations. For these reasons it is worth discussing possible methods of giving bad news at some length. Some of the ideas in this section come from articles by Maguire and Faulkener (1988a; 1988b) and Brewin (1991) and the book by Buckman (1992). Specific ways of breaking bad news to the parents of ill children can be found in Davis (1993).

Giving bad news requires flexibility. You must adjust the content of what you say and the speed at which you say it according to your assessment of how the message is being received. The following suggestions, therefore, should be modified according to circumstances. Although I can give you some guidance about general principles, I cannot tell you exactly what to say. You may find it particularly difficult at first, because giving people unwelcome news is upsetting for both parties. Remember the principles, however, and it will become easier with experience and practice.

Set the scene. Start by making the setting as comfortable and as free from interruption as you can. Allow plenty of time. You will need all your skills of verbal and non-verbal communication to structure the session and to say whatever has to be said in a sensitive manner. Eye contact will be important as you will need to observe the patient's reactions; this will give you feedback to help you as the session progresses. Your empathic qualities will be necessary to give the patient the sense that you understand the effect your words are having.

The language and the concepts you use should be appropriate to the level of understanding of the patient. If the patient is a child, much of what you say will be directed to the parents. For some, perhaps older patients for whom diabetes occurs in the context of other illnesses, less detail might be appropriate. Whatever their age, many patients find the support of a friend or relative valuable. A friend or relative is often of practical as well as emotional help. They may remember more of the session than the patient and can remind him or her of important points later. Helpers sometimes find the presence of a third party intimidating, especially when they are uncertain of their own skills, but it is best to respect the patient's wishes where possible.

By this stage you should have a fairly clear idea in your mind of what the treatment will involve. You should also know something of the patient's social and family circumstances. You will need this information shortly when you come to plan the details of the treatment programme but it is helpful to have it now as the patient may need to call upon family or friends for emotional or practical support.

Clarify. It is helpful to start by establishing what the patient already knows and what he or she thinks is likely to happen. This draws the patient into the conversation so it becomes a discussion rather than a lecture. The knowledge you gain helps you to decide how best to proceed. You might start, therefore, by saying something like 'What have you made of the symptoms so far?'; or, 'Have you given any thought to what is happening?', and 'What kind of treatment do you think you might need?'

You can then try to establish at what pace to proceed. You might ask 'Would you like me to tell you the full details of what is going on?'; or, 'Are you the kind of person who likes to know exactly what is wrong?'

Give the diagnosis. So far, you have set the scene, found out what the patient knows and how much he or she wants to know. Now you can give the diagnosis, simply and slowly. The patient is being propelled from health to chronic illness in the space of a sentence. What is just a brief sentence for you is a sentence that lasts a lifetime for the patient. If you give too much information or give it too quickly, the transition may be too much to be accomplished without the patient feeling overwhelmed and switching off. You might say, 'The glucose tolerance test confirms that you have diabetes'; or, 'The dipstick test your family doctor did showed that there was sugar in your urine. We have done some more tests since and they show that you have developed diabetes.'

Identify the patient's reactions. You can expect a wide range of reactions, from denial to confirmation of suspicions; from anger to relief. You can also expect reactions to vary in their severity, from apparent calmness to an open display of strong feelings. Therefore, when you have given the diagnosis, pause. Give the patient time to take stock and give yourself time to observe the effects of your words. If necessary, probe for a better understanding: 'How does this news leave you feeling?'; or, 'I can see that you look distressed.' It is important to identify and acknowledge any particular worries or fears before moving on, otherwise they may dominate the patient's thoughts and anything that you say subsequently may be misunderstood or only half heard.

Check the patient's understanding. It is important to check the effects your words are having as you go along because it is easy to confuse patients. Even simple words can be interpreted quite differently by different people. If you say that diabetes is a chronic disease, some will understand this to mean lifelong, but to others it can mean a disease that runs a progressive, deteriorating, course leading to infirmity and complete loss of independence. If you say that diabetes cannot be cured, some will interpret this as a death sentence. Do not assume that what a patient hears is the same as what you say. You can ask for questions, or you can say something like: 'Would you like me to explain that more clearly?'

Any questions that the patient raises should be dealt with honestly but briefly and non-technically. This is not the time to start intensive education or training. This is the time to begin to give the patient the broad framework of the treatment programme: 'We can teach you ways to control your blood sugar'; or, 'The dietitian can help you plan a healthy and varied diet'; and 'The nurse will show you how to measure your blood sugar so you can do it yourself.'

Plan for the immediate future. Next, you need to agree on immediate follow-up plans. The frequency of follow-up and the staff involved will partly depend upon medical considerations and the nature of the treatment programme. It will also depend upon the patient's family circumstances and social support, and, most importantly, the confidence of the patient and immediate family members to cope in the immediate short-term. The greater the changes that the treatment requires and the more the impact the diagnosis has had, the greater will be the need for close support. Follow-up plans should be clear and explicit. If the patient or parent is clearly upset, find out if a friend or relative is available who can offer immediate support over the next few hours and days. Find out, too, what they are going to do when they get home; sitting alone and fretting is not helpful.

Summarize. A summary at the end of the session helps cement what has been said and what the agreed follow-up arrangements are. A summary should include what the patient is going to do next and what you are going to do: 'You're going to the pharmacy to collect your tablets on the way home. I will arrange for the dietitian to see you on Wednesday so you can start planning a diet that suits you and your family. I would like to see you in clinic myself in two weeks' time.'

How Not to Break Bad News

'Well, Mr Smith, I'm afraid there's no doubt about it, your wife has definitely left you . . . yes, with your neighbour . . .no, no of course she won't come back. You can take it from me that the infidelity is permanent. It really is amazing how quickly you'll get used to the idea, especially when we've arranged some nice cookery classes for you . . .'

(Tattersall and Gale, 1990)

A number of techniques that are sometimes used are counter-productive and best avoided. No one likes giving bad news, and inappropriate ways of doing it are usually those that try to preserve the helper's own emotional equilibrium, but at the expense of the patient's. One such method is justified by the assertion that bad news is bad news however much you sugar-coat it. The patient is bound to be upset, so you should buckle down and get it over with. You set your jaw, look them straight in the eye (or avoid eye contact altogether) and come straight to the point. The patient who is psychologically unprepared tries to listen but hears nothing. This is not a good start to a professional relationship that may extend over many years.

Another approach is the bright and breezy one parodied in the quotation given at the start of this section. You cheer the patient along in your best paternalistic manner. Here you are dictating the pace and bypassing any feelings that the patient might try to discuss. The patient is a passive victim of your enthusiasm and gets left far behind.

Yet another way is to be grave and solemn, refusing to paint a positive picture for fear of being proved wrong or raising false optimism. So you recite the plain, bald facts, leaving the patient to make whatever they can of them. This will not be much, because you have behaved intellectually, and the patient's immediate response to bad news will almost certainly be largely emotional.

To remind you of the correct way, the steps are:

- set the scene;
- start by clarifying;
- give the diagnosis;
- identify the patient's reactions;

- check the patient's understanding;
- plan for the immediate future;
- summarize.

There is one more thing to do.

Talk to your colleagues. Good channels of communication between members of the care team are crucial. This is never more true than following diagnosis. Patients may be seeing a physician, dietitian, specialist nurse and possibly others in close succession. This is tiring and potentially confusing. The last thing a patient needs is for each member of the team to cover substantially the same ground but for each to give a slightly different slant or emphasis. They certainly do not need contradictory information. A classic example of this is when the physician and the nurse each recount a slightly different target figure for desirable blood glucose. Later, the patient visits their doctor and is given an entirely different figure. Information that is passed between team members should include relevant details of psychological reactions and social circumstances. It should not be limited to technical matters such as units of insulin or grammes of carbohydrate.

Adjustment and change

Before discussing some specific types of circumstance where you can help, I want to discuss two general factors that play a major part in determining how people cope with change. One is the availability of social support and the other is a person's level of self-esteem. When self-esteem is low and the patient is socially isolated or feels him- or herself to be unsupported, all adjustments are harder to make and all difficulties are magnified.

Mobilize support

For most of us, problems are easier to face and to master when other people are available to offer support and help. Support can take different forms; it can be practical, or it can be emotional. Often it is both at the same time. A partner who helps with meal planning and preparation or who prompts when medication is due is providing direct practical support. Parents who avoid eating sweets in front of their child who has diabetes, or who make sure that all the family eat the same sort of diet are also giving practical support. Such actions also have an emotional aspect because they help to make the recipient feel loved and valued.

All helpers are able to provide support, both practical and emotional. Giving information and teaching skills are practical supports. Lending a sympathetic ear, offering time and understanding, curbing any temptation to react negatively or critically when things go wrong are all powerful forms of emotional support that you will regularly use.

Support does not mean the same thing to everyone. Remember that it is something that the patient experiences rather than something that you necessarily have to do. You might set out to be supportive, but your actions or intentions might be interpreted as interfering and intrusive. This is a common experience in families with growing youngsters who are trying to develop autonomy and independence. You may need to help parents to understand that support sometimes means masterly inactivity – waiting in the wings rather than doing anything more energetic. For your part, you will often find yourself in the same position: supporting parents or patients by listening, understanding or by simply being available on the end of a telephone line when needed. For this reason, although you can offer support, you cannot impose it.

Sometimes you can help by organizing support from other patients. One possibility is to set up a buddy system whereby an 'established' patient helps someone who is newly diagnosed. Having a suitable patient available at the right time is not always possible, but worth bearing in mind. You might consider setting up support groups. There are many ways this can be done, ranging from informal social gatherings to more formal groups using counselling and group therapy techniques.

Groups can be set up that combine support with some other function, such as education. National associations, such as the British Diabetic Association and the American Diabetes Association organize a variety of supportive and educative facilities, such as family weekends and activity holidays. They are supportive because they allow participants to sample social and recreational experiences in a safe environment. They allow discussion of feelings and reactions to diabetes to take place, enabling patients to learn that while in one sense their experiences are unique, in another they are shared by others. The slogan 'You can't do it alone but you alone can do it' sums up the underlying spirit. (If you are interested in setting up a support group, you will find the book by Nichols and Jenkinson [1991] very helpful.)

Build and maintain self-esteem

We each have a picture of the sort of person we think we are and how we would like to be. If there is a gap between the way we see ourselves and the way we would like to be, self-esteem will be low. If the gap is small, we will feel good about ourselves and be self-confident and tolerant of our shortcomings. Self-esteem is made up of many components, from all the areas of life that are important to us: social functioning, performance at work or school, interpersonal relationships, and leisure activities. Since diabetes can affect all these, it is easy to see how having diabetes can have important effects on self-esteem:

> *'Self-esteem enables the patient to assume an active role in controlling care...Patients with high self-esteem feel that they are worth the time and effort needed to maintain and improve health and eagerly take responsibility to meet self-care needs. Conversely, individuals with low self-esteem may be unable to make self-care decisions and assume responsibility for care outcomes.'*
> (Miller, 1983)

You will get a good idea of how patients feel about themselves from using your skills of active listening. In particular, note any self-disparaging comments or remarks that indicate feeling insignificant or worthless. People often use jokes to say painful things about themselves while appearing to make light of them: 'Did you hear about the vampire with a sweet-tooth who only attacked badly controlled diabetics? He'd make a feast out of me!' Keep a lookout for black humour and ask direct questions: 'How has having diabetes influenced the way you feel about yourself?'; or, 'How has diabetes changed your social confidence?'

When self-esteem is low, you can help build it up. There are a number of ways of doing this.

Treat patients with respect. This can be done by using both verbal and non-verbal skills, by displaying an interest in the patient's opinions, by being less directive during a session, and by avoiding disapproval and value judgements.

Identify insensitive clinic practices. Are there ways in which your service diminishes patients' self-respect and individuality? Perhaps they have their routine eye test performed in the corridor in full view of everyone; perhaps they are weighed on arrival and have the result proclaimed for all to hear ('Up again from last time I'm afraid, Mrs Smith'.) Perhaps before being taken away for analysis, the urine samples are lined up on the receptionist's desk for all to see? Perhaps the appointment letters you send out are computer-generated, complete with hospital reference numbers, consultant code and full forenames on the address label? If so, can you redesign them? When they receive letters, patients like to feel that they have come from one human being writing to another, not from a computer interfacing with a post code.

Identify strengths. It is worth taking every opportunity to identify and praise what patients do well, rather than just working on areas where improvement can be made. Most of us find it easier to concentrate upon problems and deficits rather than upon skills and strengths, so focusing on positive qualities and achievements can be difficult for some patients. To help, you can use a sentence completion exercise. You can do this verbally during a session, or it can be done on paper as a sort of homework assignment between sessions. The idea is that you provide the first part of a sentence and the patient has to provide the second. The following would be suitable starters for patients to complete:

- 'One thing I like about myself is . . .'
- 'One thing I do very well is . . .'
- 'A problem I handled well recently is . . .'
- 'A compliment that has been paid to me recently is . . .'
- 'A temptation I overcame recently is . . .'

You can then talk through the answers and discuss what they have discovered about themselves. In this way patients learn to think positively about themselves and about specific achievements concerning their diabetes, or themselves in general. The method probably comes more naturally to children and adolescents who feel less self-conscious than adults, but it can be used with patients of any age. (If you find this sort of approach helpful, or you would like to read more about it, the book by MacLean and Oram [1988] contains a number of techniques that are suitable for use with individual patients or discussions in small groups.)

Provide experiences of success. Confidence comes from doing something successfully. Making the goals of the treatment programme realistic and achievable is the best way of doing this. I shall have more to say about this in the next chapter. It is important not to make patients feel a failure if they are unable to meet a treatment target, or if they are having a particularly difficult time with their disease. For example, if a patient is unable to cope with an intensive regimen and reverts to one that is less demanding, it is important to convey the message that the treatment was inappropriate for the patient, rather than the patient was not up to the treatment.

Encourage learning from others. Learning from other patients, rather than having to rely on traditional authority figures such as hospital staff helps people improve self-confidence. So too does the realization that they can be of help and value to others who are in similar circumstances. This is another reason why discussion groups or support groups can be of great help.

Modify self-beliefs. It is common for people to hold beliefs that make them feel bad about themselves. People are often very good at taking the blame or responsibility when things go wrong, while explaining away the good things that they do. In effect, patients may think: 'When my blood sugar is under control it is because the treatment is effective. When it is poor it is because I'm not trying hard enough.' Be on the lookout for beliefs such as this and be alert for patients who conclude that their difficulties are caused by deeply-rooted personal defects. Examples of this are the patient who says 'I'm overweight because I haven't got the will-power to diet', and the child who says 'I'm useless at keeping my blood sugar down. I'm just useless, full stop.' Sweeping statements like these, and ones that indicate that improvement is unlikely, such as 'I'm fat now and I'll always be fat', lead to poor self-esteem.

In situations such as these try to encourage the patient to be more specific and less global in their remarks: 'I might be overweight now, but with support from my family and dietitian I have a good chance of losing weight.' You can encourage patients to replace thoughts such as 'I had that slice of cake, what a failure I am' with more positive thoughts: 'I managed to stop after one slice when it could have been two. What a great job I did in stopping.'

Another method involves what is called refocusing. If you can take the emphasis away from negative thoughts, it helps to put them into perspective. This is especially true if they can be contrasted with evidence of strengths or successes. You can encourage patients to modify the things they say to themselves like this: 'I may have problems with my weight, but my blood glucose control is good'; or, 'I may be small for my age, but I do really well at my school work.' The list of personal strengths that you generated earlier can be used here.

Techniques such as these that aim to modify the judgements that people make about themselves, their expectations and their attributions, are generally described as forms of cognitive behaviour therapy. (There are many books on cognitive behaviour therapy. One that is easy to read is by Trower, Casey and Dryden [1988].)

When Changes are Predictable

Many of the changes that people go through during their lives can be anticipated. It is possible, therefore, at least to some extent to be prepared for them. This is important because changes are usually stressful. This is because they challenge the relevance of our beliefs and opinions; they require us to develop new skills or new attitudes; and they put our self-confidence to the test. When we are under stress our physiology alters and stress hormones are released as part of the well-known fight-or-flight response. Physiological changes are of particular relevance to people with diabetes because stress hormones, such as adrenaline, oppose the action of insulin and can cause destabilization of blood glucose control. People under stress also behave differently, and self-management tasks are less likely to be performed so diligently. Anticipation and preparation can reduce the impact of stressful events: forewarned is forearmed.

One young patient came home from college at the end of his first term and said this:

> *'When I went to college I found it very difficult to settle. I didn't want to tell everyone that I was diabetic. Not that I was ashamed or anything, I just didn't want to be treated any differently to the others. Everyone was eating at odd hours and staying up half the night chatting and that didn't suit my routine at all. I felt quite excluded and began to feel really angry about being diabetic, although I knew it was stupid. I started to miss some injections, but I just felt guilty. I didn't know what to do. It was on my mind all the time. My blood sugar was high all the time.'*

Going away to college is a typical example of a predictable change. Others might include changing a job, becoming a parent, or even going on holiday. All these can present real difficulties, especially to a recently diagnosed patient, or to a family where experience of living with diabetes is limited, or where confidence is low. There are a number of ways in which you can help patients.

Anticipate it. If you can predict that a situation is about to happen, you can discuss likely difficulties that might arise. In this example, a discussion with the young man before going to college would have included emotional aspects, such as living away from home for the first time and losing the support, comfort and predictability of family life and established routines. It would be helpful to probe for any more specific concerns that he might have, such as the fear of being taken ill, the stressful effects of making new relationships or something as basic as: 'Who are you going to tell about your diabetes?' Discussions should also cover practical issues, such as changes in lifestyle, new study schedules, eating routines, activity and sleep patterns and their potential impact upon diabetes.

Prepare for it. Once a potential problem has been identified, ways of dealing with it can be explored. This might involve drawing up provisional plans for day-by-day activities. It might involve making changes to the regimen. It might include identifying ways of obtaining practical and emotional support: what will he do if confidence begins to slip and things appear to be spiralling out of control? Is there a contact name for the local diabetes service? Should he make himself known to the student health service as soon as possible? Should he confide in his personal tutor? Is it appropriate for you to provide long-distance telephone support if required? Knowing what other people have found helpful and how they reacted in similar circumstances is often valuable, because this gives practical tips and puts the patient's own experiences and expectations in context.

In some circumstances specific new skills might be useful. For example, relaxation training is a positive means of coping with stress, and has many applications in day-to-day life. Relaxation is valuable because it decreases physiological arousal and leads to feelings of well-being, as well as of being in control. Relaxation is a skill that has to be learned through practice. The simplest method involves systematic muscular relaxation (instructions for this are given by Bennett [1993] in a companion volume to this book). A cassette tape of pre-recorded instructions can be a valuable tool. Such tapes are readily available and patients can be taught how to use them.

Learn from previous experiences. People tend to react to changes and stresses in ways that are characteristic of them. A discussion of how the patient reacted to past difficulties will help increase his understanding of himself and his strengths and limits. There may not be an identical experience, but there will certainly be similar situations from which to learn. The young man I quoted earlier will not have been to college before, but he may have been on holiday with the school, had difficulties planning homework assignments, or taken a long time to settle in at a new school. Your task is to help him to identify his own coping skills, and to help generate new ones. You could ask: 'What normally works for you when you're having a difficult time of things?'; or, 'How do you normally react to changes and new situations like this?'; or, 'What sorts of things tend to be particularly hard for you?'; and then, 'Building on your earlier experiences, what ways can you suggest that might be helpful in this situation?'

Debrief. If circumstances allow, talking through a situation afterwards is valuable. It helps identify what the patient did well, and so boosts self-confidence. It also identifies areas where further work is necessary. You might ask: 'What did you do that you are particularly proud of?'; and, 'How might you do it differently if a similar situation happened to you again?'; or, 'What lessons have you learned that might be useful in future?'

When Changes Are Unpredictable

Not all situations can be anticipated and plans made for them. Crises occur and the unexpected can happen in any area of a person's life at any time. The presence of diabetes is a complicating factor in the resolution of such upheavals. What I wish to discuss are the uncertainties connected with the disease itself as these present the patient, and you, with particular difficulties. I shall consider two examples to give you an idea of what I mean.

The first concerns a patient who has developed severe degenerative complications, and who has trouble coping with his changed circumstances. At best the future seems bleak; at worst, it seems very short. Activities are restricted and the quality of life is dramatically diminished. The patient feels unwell all the time and experiences powerful reactions such as anger, bitterness and despair. In this example, the patient was undergoing regular dialysis for serious kidney problems and was waiting for a kidney transplant. He was still at work for short spells, but felt that he was being carried by his workmates.

For his recent birthday the patient's wife had given him a mobile telephone so that if a kidney became available he could be contacted immediately. He arrived for the first session with the telephone hanging conspicuously from a leather holster attached to his belt. As he sat down, he adjusted the phone in a very obvious manner. After a few opening exchanges, during which he constantly toyed with the telephone, the helper decided to respond to this non-verbal hint and to use it as an opening to discuss the patient's concerns:

Helper: *'I wonder what it feels like, carrying that phone around with you all the time?'*

Patient: *'I'm not sure whether I want it to ring or whether I hope it won't.'*

Helper: *'I see; each would bring its own problems?'* (Helper makes tentative reformulation.)

Patient: *'Yes, and the uncertainty is getting me down.'* (sighs)

Helper: *'Can you bear to talk about it?'* (Patient nods, but says nothing.) *'I can see it's very difficult for you. Can you tell me what's on your mind the most?'* (Helper acknowledges feelings and seeks clarification.)

Patient: *'I feel helpless not knowing what will happen. I don't even know what I want to happen.'*

Helper: *'No wonder you feel so powerless and confused. Let's look at the alternatives. Suppose it does ring. What would be on your mind then?'* (Helper makes empathic response and seeks clarification.)

Patient: *'That the operation would fail and my wife would be left alone.'*

Helper: *'Do you have any other worries about the transplant?'* (Helper probes for further detail.)

Patient: *'That's enough, isn't it?'*

Helper: *'Yes, of course. I'd like to come back to that later, but first, let's talk about the possibility that it will never ring. What would be uppermost in your mind then?'* (Further exploration.)

In this way the helper breaks the situation down into a number of separate concerns and isolates individual worries. By making empathic responses and acknowledging feelings, the helper reduces the impact of uncertainty. Such responses do not take it away, but they legitimize it; this helps the patient to feel he is understood. The helper is then able to move on to discuss the worries one by one.

The second example of uncertainty concerns the situation where you cannot be clear or precise about what will happen. Situations like these are common: the pregnant woman who asks if her pregnancy will be normal, and the newly diagnosed adult who asks if their children will develop diabetes are both asking questions to which there are no definitive answers. I think that you can expect direct questions like these to increase in years to come, largely because of the move to involve patients more in their own care. As patients become more knowledgeable, the questions they ask become more pertinent and more difficult to answer. Recent publicity concerning the possible loss of warning symptoms of hypoglycaemia following the introduction of human insulin, and the attention that the results of the Diabetes and Complications Trial have received probably means that patients will be asking you questions that are hard to answer.

Imagine you are talking to a patient who has just had their annual eye check with the retinal camera. The results show early retinopathy. You have told the patient this, using the scheme for breaking bad news I presented at the start of the chapter. Naturally, however, the patient is still very concerned, and asks: 'What are the chances that I will go blind?' What are you to say? Do you simply give a probability estimate based upon the latest research findings? Do you make blithe soothing noises? Do you steer well clear of a potentially distressing conversation by saying: 'That's a matter for the other doctor?' Is there a better way?

As usual, it is important to understand the patient's concerns before rushing in with information or reassurance that might be premature and misplaced. So, a general, open question such as 'What have you been thinking about that?'; or, 'What worries you most about it?' would be an appropriate start. You can then indicate the general level of risk and acknowledge that this is vague. You can then try and deal with the difficulties that this might cause: 'I'm afraid I can't give a clearer answer to your question. Hearing me say that must be difficult for you.' You then move on to give clear and explicit guidance about how the risk can be reduced: 'We know that eye problems can often be stopped and sometimes reversed by good control. Would you like to talk about how we can help you lower your blood glucose?'

You may, of course, have no idea what the outlook is because, for example, you are a chiropodist or psychologist and know little about microvascular complications. It would be going beyond your competence to enter into a technical discussion. Rather than close the conversation down, however, you can acknowledge your own ignorance while still making yourself available to offer a listening, understanding ear: 'I'm afraid I don't know the answer to that question because it's not my field, but it sounds as if you're worried. Would it help to talk about your worries?'

Responses to avoid. You could say 'Diabetes is one of the commonest causes of blindness in adults.' This is true, but hardly helpful because it raises anxiety levels and does not give the patient useful information about how to reduce their personal risk. It is the sort of opening sentence you might put on a grant application form if you were applying for research funds to investigate retinopathy, but it is quite out of place in a clinic.

You could say 'Many people show proliferative retinopathy after a lifetime of diabetes. You can minimize the chances of developing further visual impairment by endeavouring to maintain normoglycaemia at all times. Nowadays, laser coagulation therapy is a very effective management technique.' All of this is true. It is also tedious, patronizing, possibly incomprehensible, and contrary to the skills discussed in Chapter Five.

Sometimes you may be tempted to give an unjustifiably precise answer rather than admit to uncertainty or ignorance. This solves nothing and may cause additional problems for patients and their families. Everyone will be familiar with stories of patients who have been given six months to live, only to confound everyone by carrying on for years. Giving 'guesstimates' of this sort is always inappropriate. As far as retinopathy is concerned, it is inappropriate because we do not know the future. Ways of achieving good blood glucose control are constantly improving, so that the prevalence figures we have now will be hopelessly out of date shortly. In addition, the data refer to statistical risk, rather than the risk to a particular individual. If health deteriorates quicker than expected, people feel cheated out of the things they have planned. If things progress slower than you have predicted, people may have withdrawn unnecessarily from their various activities and will feel frustrated. In either case, they can justifiably claim to have been misled.

Concluding Remarks

Developing diabetes is a bit like entering into an arranged marriage from which there can be no divorce or separation. Most patients can look forward to periods of amicable coexistence with their diabetes, but also to periods of disharmony and uncertainty. Just as people with marital problems may seek the services of a mediator or counsellor, one of the important functions of any helper is to act in a similar capacity to patients and their diabetes. It would be unwise to push this analogy too far because as a health worker you can do a great deal to prevent adjustment problems from starting in the first place. An important part of your job is to care for patients through a lifetime of diabetes, through periods of stress, change and uncertainty and, it must be said, through the periods of routine and tedium in between.

In this chapter I have tried to show how this can be done effectively. It has to be allied to specific ways of helping patients with their self-management tasks, which is the subject of the next chapter.

Summary

❏ The key to giving bad news is to do it at a pace that is comfortable to the patient. Taking things too fast or going into too much detail too soon leads to heightened anxiety and confusion.

❏ When giving bad news, the steps to follow are:
- set the scene;
- start by clarifying what the patient already knows;
- give the diagnosis;
- identify the patient's reactions;
- check the patient's understanding;
- make clear plans and follow-up arrangements;
- summarize.

❏ Patients will experience many changes during their lives that will affect their adjustment to diabetes and the disease itself.

❏ Support helps people to cope with the stress of change. You can provide support yourself, or facilitate support from others.

❏ Self-esteem plays a large part in determining adjustment. You can boost self-esteem by ways that include:
- treating patients with respect;
- removing insensitive clinic procedures;
- helping patients to identify their personal strengths;
- designing the treatment programme so that the patient experiences success, not failure;
- helping patients modify any self-defeating thoughts and beliefs.

❏ Many life changes are predictable. When they can be anticipated they can be discussed and plans made to reduce their potential impact.

❏ Living with diabetes means living with uncertainties, day-by-day and in the longer term. You can help patients to cope with uncertainty by acknowledging the stress of uncertainty, and by using counselling skills to understand the nature of their concerns and begin to work towards their reduction.

7

Counselling and Self-Management

In this chapter I shall discuss the use of counselling and communication skills to help patients carry out self-management tasks. Because the treatment of diabetes is largely by self-management, you need to know how to help patients understand their regimen; how to agree management goals with them; how to help them make the necessary changes to their behaviour or lifestyle; and how to support them when they run into difficulties. One of the fundamental requirements that all patients have is for information about the disease and its management. I shall start, therefore, by discussing the best ways of giving information. I introduced this topic briefly in the previous chapter when discussing ways of giving the diagnosis. Now, I shall cover it in more detail.

Giving Information

If people are to play a full part in their own treatment and make informed decisions they need the appropriate information. If they are to feel in control of themselves and their disease they need information about what to do and why they are supposed to do it. Giving a piece of information or an explanation is not just a matter of transmitting items of data. Done correctly, it gives people confidence and reduces anxiety and uncertainty; done badly, it leaves people feeling confused, bewildered and powerless:

'On one of my visits to the neurologist, he left me to get dressed in the examination room while he went back to the other office to wash his hands. I returned to find him apparently talking to his bar of soap. I remember thinking that this was a bit odd, when I realized that, far from talking to his soap he was, in fact, giving me the results of his examination. Hearing the results of an examination must be the most important part of a consultation, yet here I was being told the Great Man's opinion while he was in eye contact with a wash basin. Surely, there must be better ways of giving information that do not depend upon the ready availability of soap and water?'

Indeed there are. The sequence to try and follow is:

* be clear about why you are giving the information;
* find out what the patient already knows;
* give the appropriate information in an effective manner;
* check that the information has been understood.

Why are you giving the information?

When you set out to give information to a patient, whether it is part of an educational programme or of ongoing care, you should be clear *why* you are giving it. You should have clear aims in mind. For example, if you are a dietitian and want to tell a patient about high-carbohydrate, low-fat diets, you will have to present the same basic content in different ways according to your specific aims. Is your aim to alter the eating patterns of the patient alone, or of the whole family? Are you going to concentrate upon changing actual eating behaviour itself, or is your initial purpose to introduce the idea of healthy eating and to modify the patient's attitudes towards it? Are you giving fresh information, or attempting to correct out-dated information? If the patient is someone who has been diagnosed recently and knows little about diets, a different approach will be required compared to someone with a long experience of diabetes who has seen almost every possible combination of carbohydrate, fat and protein recommended over the years.

Information is important, but it is not the answer to everything. It is necessary for self-management, but it is not sufficient. If you are a dietitian, you will probably have noticed that some of the most over-weight people you meet are also some of the most knowledgeable about diets. Helpers from other professions will have no difficulty in providing similar examples from their area of work. This means that once a certain level of knowledge has been reached, there is little point in giving any more. If knowledge is adequate, then further information amounts to no more than a repetition of what the patient already knows. This can be frustrating for you and humiliating for the patient. In many situations the problem is not one of knowledge so much as putting that knowledge into practice. This might indicate that the problem is rather different, perhaps one of confidence or motivation rather than one of knowledge, and should be tackled appropriately. I discussed improving self-confidence in the previous chapter and will consider motivation again later. Do not assume that a problem can always be solved by information or education: ask yourself, is the information I want to give really necessary?

What does the patient already know?

Whatever you say will be understood by your patient in the context of what they already know. You need to understand this so that your message can be tailored to suit the patient's needs. You may have to fill gaps or correct misconceptions that you have identified. The best way of finding out about a patient's current knowledge or beliefs is to ask, if necessary by asking direct questions. So, a chiropodist might ask, 'What do you know about how to care for your feet?' or, 'Can you tell me why foot care is important for you?'

Take special care to assess patients who have been treated previously at other clinics. This is because clinical practice is by no means uniform. All health workers have their own favourites, whether it be an insulin or drug regimen, or a favourite diet plan. It is important not to make assumptions about what a patient who is new to your service knows. For their part, patients coming from afar will have expectations about how a clinic should be run and what sort of treatment they require. These may be quite different to your own ideas, and you will have to discuss them together: 'I imagine that you are wondering how things here will compare with your old clinic?' is a suitable opener. You can ask, 'What was good about the care you received there?'; or, 'Perhaps there were things you would have liked to have done differently?' These will help you understand your patient's perspective and expectations with greater accuracy.

How do you give information?

Here, you call into action the skills of good communication discussed in Chapter Five. There are some specific additional points to bear in mind.

Take account of the patient's age. As they mature intellectually, children are able to grasp some aspects of the regimen earlier than they can grasp others. Practical skills such as self-monitoring of blood glucose are learned and performed competently before the child is capable of understanding the reasons for doing so, or is able to modify the diet or insulin dosage rationally on the basis of the results. Some information, therefore, might be appropriately given to the child and some will have to be directed towards the parents. There is a particularly awkward time during adolescence when it is often unclear who is supposed to be doing what: is it youngster or is it parent? You will have to review the informational needs of adolescents as they develop intellectually and become more independent. In fact, you will have to review regularly all their requirements: skills, understanding and emotional support. A good way of doing this is to develop a comprehensive review system at your workplace, perhaps similar to the one described by the North Tyneside Diabetes Team (1992).

At the other end of the age range, older patients may acquire information at a slower rate and their concentration span may be reduced. Many older patients will not have had to assimilate a lot of information for a long time, since leaving school perhaps, and will be out of practice. Sessions may have to be shorter and the material paced more gently. It can be helpful to involve relatives or carers if you are concerned about the patient's ability to understand and retain the material.

Use simple language. It is important not to talk over the patient's head as this can lead to serious misunderstandings. Patients may be too embarrassed or too polite to tell you they have no idea what you are talking about. Think about the words you use, and avoid the use of jargon. Patients object to jargon because they feel excluded from the conversation. Make sure that this complaint cannot be levelled at you.

Sometimes we lapse into jargon or cliché phrases to hide the fact that we do not really mean anything at all, or to avoid real thought. When was the last time you described someone, although probably not to their face, as being a bit 'neurotic'? The word means nothing; it is a vague term of abuse. If you do use it, perhaps it is because you have not thought deeply enough about the person and have not really understood them properly. Thinking about it, you may conclude that you mean that the patient is anxious and appears to need a lot of attention and reassurance. If so, then ask yourself why the patient is anxious and so insecure that reassurance is constantly required. Stop and think through what you mean when you find yourself using jargon. Further, if you would not use certain words in front of patients, try not to use them behind their back.

Be practical. Use relevant, real-life practical examples to make your points and to assess the impact of what you have said in preference to a dry, theoretical style. Rather than ask a child 'What is the thing to do if your blood sugar is very high before taking exercise?', try saying, 'If you are about to take part in the cross-country run at school in the afternoon and your blood glucose before lunch is 12 mmol/l, what would you do?'

Consider using aids. Handouts can be useful to underline and emphasize important points. They can also be used in the patient's own time and home, and at their own pace. There is a wide range of booklets and videos from which to choose. If you use such aids, remember that they cannot be tailored to suit individual patients or your own practices and procedures. Make sure that you are familiar with them yourself, as you may need to answer questions on them later. Make sure, too, that they do not describe treatment methods that you do not use at your work-place, or give advice to which you do not subscribe.

Keep sessions short. People have a limited attention span. You will see different time limits recommended for the ideal length of a session, ranging from about 15 to 45 minutes. It is difficult to give a fixed rule as some people can absorb more information during a session than others. It depends upon other factors as well, such as the complexity of what you are saying and the emotional state of the patient. Information that is presented too quickly or in too much depth will not be retained. The important thing is to proceed at a pace that the patient finds comfortable. This is almost certainly slower than you might think. The more you try to cram in, the more will be forgotten. This is so obvious it might hardly seem worth mentioning, but it is important. Most people will stop a session when they see the patient's eyes begin to glaze, but the smart thing to do is to stop before that point is reached. 'Always leave 'em wanting more' is a slogan that applies to the clinic as much as it does to the music hall.

How much has been understood?

A good way to check for understanding is to note the patient's non-verbal behaviour. Does he or she appear riveted or bored, beaming or blank? You can ask the patient to repeat important points, and you can ask for questions. The main difficulty with asking for questions is that patients may be afraid to ask any for fear of appearing slow or stupid. You can get around this by taking the blame for potential misunderstandings yourself: 'I want to check that I explained that properly' is better than, 'I want to check that you understood what I just said.'

If you are giving some information as part of a series of sessions, such as after diagnosis or following a major change to the regimen, it is helpful to start each session by asking the patient to run over what they remember from the previous session. This is because memory is an active process. People, yourself included, modify internally what they have heard in the light of existing knowledge, attitudes and what they would like to have heard. By asking for a report you can check a patient's understanding of what was said, as well as the amount remembered. A proportion of what you say will be forgotten however well you present it, but there is a lot you can do to reduce forgetting to a minimum.

How can you reduce forgetting?

When you were a student, did you ever reach the end of a lesson and realize that you remembered nothing of what you had just been taught? If you did, you can understand how patients sometimes feel. Student or patient, a proportion of what we hear goes in one ear and out the other. When you were a student you probably blamed the teacher for bad presentation and poor delivery; now that you are a helper, make sure these accusations cannot be levelled at you and you do not blame the patient for poor motivation and bad concentration.

A number of factors affect what a patient remembers. Anxiety is one – a patient who is anxious will remember less. So too will someone who has been diagnosed recently and who is still emotionally unsettled, as well as being unfamiliar with the disease-related words and concepts that are so familiar to the professional. This is why giving much information immediately after diagnosis is inadvisable. You might think it surprising, but intelligence does not play a great role in determining how much is remembered. Very few patients are incapable of understanding the management requirements because of low intelligence. We tend to assume that highly intelligent patients will understand what we say, and, being intelligent and rational, will go straight off and act appropriately. Anyone who has worked in a student health service will know that this is not true.

The way in which you present your material will help to determine how far it is understood and remembered. There are a number of steps you can take to reduce forgetting.

Put important points first. If you put important information or advice near to the start of a session, it will be remembered more easily than if you put it towards the end, when the patient is feeling tired and is beginning to switch off.

Structure the material. It is easy to overburden patients with information and advice, especially if there is no clear link or framework holding it together. People remember more and understand better if they have a structure or framework because this reduces the demands made on memory.

Be specific. Vague instructions are difficult to remember because it is not clear what the patient is supposed to do. Avoid vague generalities such as 'Look after your feet.' Say something like 'After each bath, check your feet for damage to the skin. Make sure you dry between your toes; blot the skin with the towel, don't rub it dry.'

Emphasize important points. If something is important, say so. Do not run the risk of it being lost in the throes of everything else that happens during the session.

Repeat important points. Simply by repeating important information you will do a lot to ensure that it is remembered. If you have ever done any classroom teaching, you may have come across the advice given to lecturers to say what you are going to say, say it and then say what you have just said. So, as I just said, repetition is valuable.

The following example indicates how many of these points can be incorporated into a natural flow. Remember the patient with the visual difficulties from the previous chapter? The session might have continued like this:

Helper: *'I have examined your eyes and everything looks normal and healthy. It is important that you remember that there is no sign of eye disease.'* (Helper uses simple, clear language; emphasizes and repeats the important point; puts important information first; pauses to let the news sink in; and gives the patient the opportunity to respond.)

Patient: *'That's quite a relief.'*

Helper: *'Yes, that's good, isn't it? I think that the symptoms are caused by swings in your blood sugar levels. I can give you more details about why I think that if you would like me to.'* (Helper acknowledges the patient's reaction, involves him in deciding how much information to give, and paces the session according to the patient's preferences.)

Patient: *'No, I'll take your word for it.'*

Helper: *'So now we have to sort out why it has been swinging about so much recently. What thoughts do you have about that?* (Helper gives a signpost to the next task and involves the patient in clarification.)

If you would like to read more about giving information and about remembering and forgetting in health-care settings, then the book by Ley (1988) is a good place to start.

Making Changes and Teaching Skills

Much of diabetes management involves learning practical skills rather than accumulating theoretical knowledge. Injection technique, foot care and self-monitoring are obvious examples. There are many less obvious situations. Choosing a buffet meal in a restaurant or hotel dining-room is as much a practical skill as it is an exercise in remembering the carbohydrate content of the foods the patient is likely to meet. It is all very well remembering from your reading that 40gms of boiled brown rice contain 10gms of carbohydrate, but the important practical question is, how big a heap does that make on your plate? For a child, being able to say 'no' to grandmother, who is plying you with sweets, is a practical skill; it is also a matter of confidence. The patient will almost certainly know that eating a bag of sweets is not a good idea, but the ability to put that knowledge into practice without giving offence is a different matter altogether.

If you wanted to learn how to drive a car you would not just lie on the sofa and read a book about it. Nor would you go to an instructor who was genuine and empathic but who failed to give you specific instructions and detailed feedback about your performance. Instead, you would go to someone who would tell you which pedal to press and when to press it, and who gave you plenty of opportunities for supervised practice. For a patient, much of learning to control their diabetes is like this, and the principle is the same in both cases: learning by doing. Here are some guidelines for teaching skills and modifying the treatment programme.

Agree on the goals before you start. If you do not know where you are going, how will you know when you have got there? Zen masters may tell you that the journey is more important than the destination, but they are not diabetes educators. Your goals should be clear, explicit, agreed and SMART:

Specific: 'We agree that you will measure your blood glucose every day half an hour before breakfast and before your evening meal . . .'

Measurable: '. . . and that you will record the result in your log-book.'

Achievable: 'What problems can you foresee that might get in the way of doing it?'

Relevant: 'We agree that this is important because it will help us sort out how best to adjust your medication.'

Time-limited: 'Starting tomorrow, we agree that you shall do this until our next appointment in two weeks' time.'

These are largely self-explanatory, but a little more detail might be helpful.

Specific. Be precise. Language is capable of great precision, but it is equally capable of great vagueness: 'Do you test your blood sugar regularly?' 'Oh, yes, nurse, very regularly.' Before each meal is 'regularly'. So too is every six months. If you want a patient to do something, you must give them enough detail to enable them to do it properly. It is not sufficient to say 'Take more exercise' or, 'Try to lose some weight.' Different people will have different views on what these mean, so you must be more specific. In these examples you should agree a target weight and the amount and frequency of exercise.

Measurable. Some educational efforts, especially those which rely upon verbal tuition, increase a patient's confidence without having much effect on their competence. In many ways, confident but unskilled patients are in a more vulnerable position than unskilled patients who recognize their limitations. For this reason it is best where possible to observe patients carrying out self-management tasks rather than relying exclusively upon a verbal report of their abilities.

The more explicit the goal the easier it will be to tell whether it has been reached. There are a number of ways you can assess this. You might ask a patient to select a meal containing a given amount of carbohydrate from a menu or from an array of food on a table. You might ask a patient to demonstrate correct injection technique while you compare their performance against criteria of good practice. Examples of good practice and guidelines recommended by national diabetes associations are regularly published in the main professional journals. You can, of course, develop your own criteria, and this might well be a valuable task for a local audit group.

Achievable. When agreeing goals it is better to start with something fairly modest that can be built upon and extended rather than be over-ambitious and run into problems. Early success, and the self-confidence that success brings, are important. Some patients will try to set unrealistic goals and you then have the task of negotiating something more achievable. One way of assessing whether a patient is being realistic or not is to ask what problems they foresee in trying to carry out the plan. Another way is to ask how they see themselves in a few months' time; someone who expects to lose three stone in weight in three months' time is being unrealistic. These methods will help you to agree a more realistic first target.

Relevant. The reasoning behind the programme should be clear and acceptable to the patient. When people do not see that the programme is relevant to them and the outcome worth striving for, their motivation is low and changes are not sustained.

Time-limited. You should both be clear about the time-scale for the programme. People find it much easier to work within short time-frames when trying to introduce some new self-management technique or change some aspect of their behaviour. Giving up smoking, for instance, is easier done day by day, rather than thinking that you have to abstain for the rest of your life. Similarly, it is easier to achieve a period of intensive self-monitoring successfully if working within a clear time-scale.

A wide variety of practical methods have been developed to help patients change their behaviour and acquire the skills of self-management. Many of you will realize that the things I have been discussing so far in this chapter, such as goal-setting and the gradual implementation of changes into a treatment programme, are part of behavioural psychology. If you are interested in pursuing this further, then the book by Shillitoe (1988) contains a chapter on the use of behavioural methods specifically for patients who have diabetes. The discussion covers working with all age groups, with individuals and families, and tackling problems as diverse as injection phobias and weight-loss.

Giving feedback

Feedback is an essential part of learning. There will be many times when you will need to give it: perhaps when you have just observed someone give themselves their first injection; or when you have just examined a young person's log-book of blood glucose results. The aim of giving feedback in such situations is to help patients improve their self-confidence and self-management skills. However, it is easy to give feedback in a way that is counter-productive, that makes people resistant to changing their ways and damages their confidence. You can avoid this by using the following four-point plan.

Suppose you are seeing a middle-aged woman with Type 2 diabetes who is trying, without much success, to lose weight. You have asked her to keep a record of everything she eats and drinks for one week. You now have the record and the patient in front of you.

Clarify any matters of fact. If you are unsure about anything, ask for clarification. Try to be objective and non-judgemental. You might say; 'I see you have cut down on sugar in your tea, but I notice that you still take one spoonful. Tell me more about that, please.' This is better than, 'You still take one spoonful of sugar in your tea. Why?' Terse questions sound accusatory and can put the patient on the defensive. She might have thought that she had done remarkably well to get down to one teaspoon and you have just undermined her sense of achievement.

Ask for the patient's views before giving your own. Allow her to make the first comments about the dietary record. In this way you will learn her own views about their strengths or weaknesses. It will also help her retain a feeling of control over the session, rather than being on the receiving end all the time. Suitable questions could include the following: 'What have you learned by keeping the record?' 'What are you most pleased with about your eating pattern?' 'What aspects of your diet do you think you need to look at further?'

Highlight some good points first. You should discuss her strengths and achievements first before making any suggestions. Although you are probably going to make some recommendations, not everything will need to change, so identify and comment upon the good things first. This is because feedback that emphasizes failures can easily lead to arguments and resistance. It is also very dispiriting to have your efforts greeted by criticism. Negative feedback is not very helpful. Comments could include: 'Breakfast looks fine' (explain why); or, 'I see you are eating fruit every day. That's good.'

Agree recommendations. Although you will have a view of what changes need to be made, it is better to ask for the patient's own suggestions first. This is an extension of point two in the earlier paragraph. It helps the patient think positively and shows respect for their views. It is also best if you can phrase your comments in a positive manner. It is better to say, 'It would be better to grill bacon rather than fry it, because that will help you to cut down on fat' rather than, 'You are eating too much fat. Stop frying your food.'

Recommendations also have to be specific if they are to be helpful. Feedback that is given in very global and general terms does not identify what the patient actually has to do in the future. I covered this point earlier in the chapter when I wrote of the need for precision in giving information. Recommendations should also, of course, be given at a pace with which the patient can cope. Too much feedback, however helpful, can be overwhelming. Try to end the session by agreeing specific targets to be aimed at by the next session. For example: 'So, for the next month we have agreed that you are going to try two things. One is to grill your food rather than fry it. The other is to have some fruit rather than a pudding at lunch-time every day.'

When Motivation Flags

Most people at some time in their life will have made a New Year's resolution. They will know just how easy it is for good intentions to fall by the wayside, and for old habits to reassert themselves gradually. The same applies to keeping to the treatment programme. You might think that this tendency for old ways to regain the upper hand is just a progressive decay of will-power and determination, but that is not necessarily so.

For a start, it is important to appreciate that patients may be quite ambivalent about keeping to the management tasks. Intellectually a patient may know that self-care is important in the long-term but in everyday life, powerful pressures may be acting in quite the opposite direction. Self-monitoring may be inconvenient, exercise may seem like a chore, and not eating cakes or sweets may be felt to be a deprivation. There are very few immediate rewards to be had from keeping to the management programme – but quite a number from abandoning it. It is hardly surprising that patients often become fed up with all the restrictions and limitations and make an active decision to throw self-control to the winds for a time. 'I know all about healthy eating' one youngster told me as he tucked into a large portion of French fries.

This does not mean that patients are simply the passive victims of their emotions and circumstances. It means that at that moment they have chosen to behave in that particular way. They might regret it later but at the time it is easier to give in rather than resist, and so the decision is made to flow with the tide rather than anchor against it. There are a number of steps you can take to help patients resist such pressures.

Treat patients with respect. You should recognize this heading by now; it is the third time I have used it. You are there to be constructive and supportive. It is not your job to sit in judgement, to condemn or confer absolution.

Be open. It is important to be open about discussing with the patient any difficulties that occur or any troublesome circumstances that lie ahead. It is much better to do this than enter into a conspiracy of silence and pretend that difficulties will not happen. I wrote about preparing for predictable stresses and crises in the previous chapter, and this is one further aspect of it. Temptations ('That looks nice, one piece of cake won't harm me') and social pressures ('Come on, just this once'), are seldom far away. Negative emotions such as frustration, anger or even tiredness are constant potential sources of difficulty.

Helpers often feel ill-at-ease when discussing possible problems. For example, you might fear that by talking about times when the patient will not feel like dietary restraint you might be planting the seed of relapse in the patient's mind, perhaps almost giving permission for uncontrolled eating to occur.

Yet, to prepare for problems does not increase the chances of them occurring. To be insured against fire means that the possibility has been prepared for, but it does not make us more careless with matches; when the cabin crew on an aircraft demonstrate the life-jackets before take-off, the pilot does not become more negligent when flying over water. Patients need a relapse drill in which helper and patient jointly prepare for likely difficulties. Identifying high-risk situations is the first stage. You can ask 'What problems are you likely to face?'; and, 'When are these likely to be the hardest to handle?' Because people usually know themselves well, they will probably tell you. You can then prepare plans for what to do as and when the situations arise, as discussed in the previous chapter.

Encourage ownership of the treatment programme. When patients see themselves as being responsible for aspects of the programme, it is more likely that they will be maintained. When they feel that they have been imposed upon them by outside forces (i.e. you) the relevant behaviour is less robust and more vulnerable to problems. If they are imposed from outside, then you also perpetuate the belief that you have all the answers and the patient's self-determination and self-esteem suffers. Management decisions should be personal choices facilitated by the helper. One way of doing this is to ask for and encourage any statement that acknowledges the need for change: 'What things have you noticed about your control that concern you?'; 'What aspects of the treatment programme do you think need more attention?' Notice that leading questions can be deliberately used to create the expectation that change is indicated.

It is also helpful to concentrate upon positive reasons for keeping to the programme. If self-management is simply to avoid unpleasant things, motivation tends to be short-lived. It is much better to identify positive reasons for doing so and to work towards those. For an obese person such positive reasons may vary from wanting to be able to wear fashionable clothes to wanting to feel good about themselves. Such reasons are like incentives. They are very personal and what is effective for one person will leave another one quite unmoved. To help people begin to think about what is important for them you can ask general questions, such as 'In what ways would things be better if ...?' or, 'What would be good about ...?' You can be more specific: 'What would the family appreciate by ...?' or, 'How would things be better at work if ...?'

Techniques to avoid

Persuasion. ('Why don't you ...') Is it possible to persuade patients to change by force of argument? In theory yes, but in practice persuasion is rarely effective:

Helper: *'Have you thought about trying to lose weight?'*

Patient: *'Yes, but it's not easy, is it?'*

Helper: *'No, but you would feel a lot better if you were slimmer and we could probably cut down on your insulin.'*

Patient: *'Yes, but I always feel worse when I'm dieting. And I don't mind the injections now.'*

Helper: *'But your blood pressure would come down and that would be good, wouldn't it?'*

Patient: *'Yes, but I'd rather feel good now. Besides, we've all got to die of something, haven't we?'*

Helper: *'Yes, but ... See you in six months, then.'* (Thinks: I'll be on holiday, but the new registrar can have a go.)

One very real danger, as this made-up conversation demonstrates, is that attempts to persuade people to change can easily end up in frustrating arguments. This is because patients feel pushed into defending their actions. They feel obliged, as you would in their shoes, to emphasize how hard they have tried, to point out how difficult the diet is, how expensive, how it clashes with the eating preferences of the rest of the family, how hungry they feel, and how helpless they are in the face of all these problems. It seems obvious that anything that forces the patient to justify their failure will make the situation worse, because as people defend a position they become more and more committed to it and more and more resistant to change. If you doubt this, try to recall the last time you heard anybody modify their views during a political debate. Yet in the heat of the clinical moment helpers can easily fall into this trap. Every time you behave as an authority figure you are increasing the chances that the patient's behaviour will continue as a reaction against the threats that you have just issued to their autonomy and right to self-determination.

Next time you hear yourself say 'Yes, but ...', or, 'No, but ...' the alarm-bells should begin to ring. Your words might be about to have the opposite effect to what you intend. Every time you hear patients justifying their behaviour and telling you all the reasons why they have not done or can not do certain things, be prepared to draw back in order to avoid confrontation.

Fear arousal. ('If you don't do as I say ...') It is only a short step from trying to persuade or cajole people into following advice to trying to frighten them into submission:

Helper: *'Had you thought about what might happen if your blood glucose stays as high as this?'*

Patient: *'You mean complications?'*

Helper: *'Yes. You might go blind. Not only that, the circulation to your lower limbs may become impaired, so that if you cut your foot it might get infected, become gangrenous and require amputation.'*

It is unlikely that many helpers are as blatant as the one in this fictitious example, and most would deny with indignation ever using fear as a weapon. However, subtle forms are often used without realizing it. A phrase such as 'If you don't look after yourself ...' might sound harmless, but it contains an implicit threat. Phrases even as mild as this should be used with caution. Never make a patient feel frightened or vulnerable.

Fear arousal is a technique to avoid for two reasons. First, it can strengthen the problem it is trying to weaken. This is because powerful threats can bring about strong feelings of anxiety and helplessness. The patient feels even more trapped in the very behaviour they are being advised to change. To be effective a threat has to appear to be realistic, but if complications and early death are seen as being well-nigh inevitable and unavoidable, what is the point of striving for good control? Given such gloomy future prospects many patients will chose the good life now, and it is very difficult to counter such a decision:

Patient: *'Are all those terrible things definitely going to happen to me?'*

Helper: *'Not necessarily, but you run a much greater extra risk.'*
Patient: *'A short life but a merry one, eh?'*
Helper: *'Well, yes, but . . .'*

Second, although it can be effective in the short-term (drink-and-drive campaigns at Christmas-time are usually based on fear arousal), it is necessary to keep raising the level of threat if it is to retain longer-term effectiveness. This rapidly becomes impossible to sustain. There may be some patients who will respond to being frightened into appropriate action, but there is no easy way to identify them and you will harm more people than you help. Not only that, I hope it has not escaped you attention that using threats to get your way is hardly consistent with the philosophy of empowering patients.

If you do find yourself having to pick up the pieces after someone else has used scare tactics, you must try to give the patient back some feelings of power and control: 'It's true that some patients have problems with their circulation after many years of diabetes. You can do a great deal to prevent this from happening to you. One important thing you can do is . . .' and then go on to give specific advice based on their own particular circumstances.

You might think that I am labouring the point, but there is a danger that frightening messages will be given out more frequently in the future, now that there is strong evidence of a link between blood glucose control and long-term health. You should do all you can to avoid using research results as a stick to brandish in front of your patients. Better to use the findings as a carrot: that good control definitely results in better health.

Concluding Remarks

One way to empower patients with diabetes is to give them the information and the skills to manage the disease themselves. In this chapter I have discussed effective ways of doing this. Giving patients self-management skills is an essential aspect of whole-person care, but remember that it must be set in context. When you encounter a patient who is having difficulties, it is tempting to try to do something practical because it gives you the feeling of being useful. Looking back, whenever I have made mistakes with patients it has generally been because I have plunged into doing something before carrying out an adequate assessment of what the patient's needs really are. This has usually been because I felt under pressure from the patient or from colleagues to get some 'treatment' under way as soon as possible. Experience shows that this is a pressure to be resisted. If you take time to use your relationship-building skills and those of counselling and communication to listen and to understand, you will be better able to offer help that is relevant and appropriate. Lack of knowledge or expertise may be part of the problem and teaching self-management skills may be part of the solution. It is usually not the whole solution. Make sure that your assessment of a patient's needs is comprehensive.

Summary

❏ Patients need information about their illness and about its treatment if they are to carry out the self-management tasks that are required of them.

❏ Information also improves confidence and reduces anxiety and uncertainty.

❏ When giving information, there are four steps:
– be clear about why you are giving the information;
– find out what the patient already knows;
– give the information using simple language, taking into account relevant factors such as the patient's age;
– check that the information has been understood;
– keep sessions short.

❏ You can increase the amount that patients remember by:
– stating important points near the start of the session;
– structuring your material into a logical format;
– being as specific as you can;
– emphasizing important points by telling the patient that they are important;
– repeating important points.

❏ When teaching a practical skill, or introducing a new management programme, be SMART: agree goals that are Specific; Measurable; Achievable; Relevant and Time-limited.

❏ Learning cannot take place without feedback. When giving feedback, the best sequence is:
– clarify any matters of fact;
– ask for the patient's views before giving your own;
– highlight some good points first;
– make recommendations, not criticisms.

There are many pressures that patients have to combat in keeping to the management programme. You can help patients by:
– treating patients with respect;
– being open;
– encouraging patients to play an active part in developing and 'owning' the programme.
– avoiding the use of persuasion or force of argument in an attempt to encourage patients to keep to the programme;
– Never making patients feel frightened or vulnerable; emphasize the positive benefits from good control rather than the dangers of poor control.

8

Developing and Delivering Whole-Person Care

In this chapter I shall examine some of the issues that arise when trying to develop a diabetes service that provides whole-person care. I shall also discuss methods of developing your own personal skills further. Although I am writing from the viewpoint of someone who works in the British health-care system, this is not to say that the issues are unique to Britain. Health services in many developed nations are undergoing rapid changes. In Britain the driving forces have been both ideological and economic and stem from central government. In the United States, by comparison, the health insurance industry is a much more powerful lobby, but it too is asking questions about costs, outcomes and value for money. Many people worry that asking these questions (or, rather, the answers that they might get) threatens the development of whole-person care. This is not necessarily true, but clinicians and planners now have to be much more aware of these issues than before.

Service Delivery

Health care policy-makers wish to develop services that are local, easily accessible, appropriate to the needs of the patients, responsive to their views and clearly evaluated. A significant problem when trying to design a comprehensive diabetes service that satisfies these criteria is the wide range of patients for which it has to cater. This extends from the very young to the very old; from the recently diagnosed to those who have had the disease for fifty years or more; from the seriously ill to those who feel, and in most respects are, fit and healthy. Some patients will require minimal contact with the service while others, including youngsters, pregnant women, patients with complications and the frail elderly, have very different needs as groups and as individuals, and require more frequent contact and active support.

Community base or hospital base?

Most patients like to be seen in familiar surroundings by staff they know well. Their GP's surgery should be able to provide this. It is often argued that GPs are in an ideal position to understand their patients as people with individual needs because family doctors are familiar with their patients' background, family and community circumstances. Practice-based care, supported by hospital-based diagnostic and treatment services when required, has been developing gradually for several years and is encouraged by new health-care funding arrangements. Others fear that such decentralization of care will lead to the absorption of patients with diabetes into general surgeries rather than specialized 'mini-clinics'. The worrying implication of this is that consultations will become brief, rushed and medically orientated, so leading to the neglect of discussions about lifestyle and psychological concerns.

Diabetes centres that serve a district population are growing in popularity. They are best thought of as a local resource, serving both care staff and patients. They provide a place where patients (and, hopefully, family members as well) can spend time to learn about diabetes and discuss needs and problems in a relatively relaxed and informal way. They make communication easier between team members. The use of clinical nurse specialists in such centres is particularly important, not only for direct patient care, but also because they can act as a link between the centre and primary care staff on the one hand, and between the centre and hospital-based staff on the other.

Traditionally, especially as far as Type 1 diabetes is concerned, care has been delivered from hospital-based clinics. In principle, hospitals should have the personnel, the facilities and the wealth and depth of experience to provide good psychological and physical care. In practice, it has often been unclear which patients benefit from attendance at a hospital clinic, and so follow-up and discharge policies have been vague. This has led to overcrowding. Patients dislike hospital clinics and often criticize them for being impersonal, inconvenient and time-consuming:

Whereas the physician is stressed through overwork, the patients are stressed through inactivity. They are bored with waiting for their consultation, invariably behind schedule, with waiting times ranging between 0.5 to 3.0 hours. The degree of lateness depends upon the ratio of physicians/patients, the efficiency and honesty of the appointments system, and the position on the waiting list (best to have an early appointment). Late consultations have several implications: being late for work, the lift-home by friend/bus/ambulance, or for the next meal. Many diabetic clinic appointment cards should contain the following health warning:

**Diabetic Clinic
Health Warning
Beware of Hypoglycaemia.
Bring lunch with you for a morning
appointment**

(Parrott, 1990)

There are clear national trends in service delivery. Particularly evident is the move to community-based services and pressure to develop more clearly defined criteria for referral to specialists when particular forms of assessment and treatment are necessary. National diabetes associations such as the British Diabetic Association and the American Diabetes Association regularly produce guidelines for specific aspects of diabetes care and publish them in their respective journals (see Appendix).

Despite this there is considerable local variability. This is not necessarily bad, because none of the forms of care delivery I have just outlined have been subject to thorough evaluation. To the question 'What is the best type of service for my locality?' there is no clear authoritative answer. Diabetes care is one of those areas where, to paraphrase Newton's Third Law of Motion, for every research finding there is an equal and opposite research finding. Furthermore, studies that evaluate services may produce findings that are appropriate for one particular locality but which may be quite inappropriate elsewhere, where there are quite different geographical and population characteristics.

The best advice I can give you is that when you read articles about delivering services, you should read them critically. It is always a sound policy to note the authors' addresses. As a rule, you will find that authors who praise hospital-based care generally have affiliations with hospitals, while those advocating community-based services always seem to have community addresses. It is wise to remember also that the organization of diabetes services, as for all health care, is as much a matter for political debate as it is for scientific investigation. Like many political debates, arguments about the best form of diabetes care generate more heat than light, and the actual evidence from which conclusions are drawn is limited.

Accepting, then, that the settings in which readers currently work, or will work in the future, will be very varied, implementing whole-person care will provide particularly local challenges. There are, however, many things you can do.

Set targets and objectives

Encourage your colleagues and managers to agree targets and objectives for diabetes care. Most areas of health care are moving towards setting targets and standards. Many diabetes services have already begun this process. Here, for example, are the quality objectives produced by the diabetes services in Sheffield, Great Britain for a newly diagnosed patient (Ward and MacKinnon, 1992). He or she should expect:

* a full medical examination;
* an explanation of what diabetes is and an outline of likely treatment;
* a session with a specialist dietitian with additional sessions depending on the nature of the patient and their particular diabetes;
* the institution of insulin treatment will require frequent sessions on a one-to-one basis, usually with a diabetes specialist nurse with a wide experience of insulin management;
* instruction and help from this nurse in monitoring diabetes, with blood glucose tests for those having insulin treatment and (probably) with urine tests for those not having insulin treatment;
* detailed practical information about problems of hypoglycaemia – the most feared complication of the disease;
* discussion about factors in daily living with regard to diabetes – namely, employment, driving, insurance, prescription charges and driving licence;
* information about the diabetes associations, both nationally and locally;
* all consultations and sessions should allow a family member or friend to accompany the person with diabetes.

The achievement of such objectives, with their emphasis on education and information, together with support for the problems of living with the disease, requires good psychological care as much as it does specialist knowledge and expertise. In the past, however, this has seldom been made explicit, and there is still a gap between the stating of objectives and their actual practical daily pursuit. The situation is beginning to change, and the St Vincent Declaration is an important step in the process. This is a document that sets out agreed international targets for diabetes care in such areas as the reduction of diabetes-related blindness, end-stage renal failure, amputation, coronary heart disease and problems associated with pregnancy.

A working party has prepared 'Guidelines for encouraging psychological well-being' as part of the St Vincent Declaration action programme (Bradley et al., 1994). The working party has defined a number of broad goals with accompanying suggestions for 'creating an environment in which psychological difficulties are less likely to develop and/or disrupt diabetes self-care and metabolic control is more readily attained'. The broad goals identified by the working party are:

- improving communication;
- protecting patients' self-esteem;
- responding to individuals' differing needs;
- helping patients learn about their own individual responses;
- helping to motivate self-care;
- monitoring of psychological well-being;
- organizational changes to optimize psychosocial aspects of diabetes care.

I hope that on reading this book you will have found many examples of how you can pursue these goals by using counselling and communication skills and of how the underlying attitude that fosters respect for patients' individuality and self-determination can be incorporated into your day-by-day working practices.

Measure psychological states

Most clinics measure physical states, such as HbA_1 and body weight, and screen for physical complications. Some assess knowledge and skills by using checklists, especially for newly diagnosed patients. You should think of trying to widen your net to measure psychological states and outcomes as well. Questionnaires have been developed to measure a wide range of psychological issues, including the psychological impact of diabetes, self-esteem, quality of life and satisfaction with treatment.

For example, a questionnaire described by its authors as an 'individualized needs assessment instrument' (Hess et al., 1986) was designed to pinpoint the impact of diabetes and to identify areas where support or intervention might be needed. This example will give you the idea:

My diabetes and its treatment keep me from:
    . . . having enough money;

  ... doing my work and other responsibilities;
  ... going out travelling as much as I want;
  ... being as active as I want;
  ... having good relationships with people;
  ... having a schedule I like (e.g. sleeping late).

Similarly, if you are interested in family support, the questionnaire by Schafer et al. (1986) might be helpful. Here is a sample question:

 How often does the family member:
  ... praise you for following your diet?
  ... nag you about testing your glucose level?
  ... help you decide if changes should be made based on glucose testing results?
  ... congratulate you for sticking to your diabetes self-care schedule?
  ... criticize you for not exercising regularly?
  ... let you sleep late rather than getting up to take your insulin?

(The whole area of the development, use and limitations of question-naires in diabetes research and practice is the subject of a forthcoming book by Bradley [1994].)

Audit your service

If you have an audit group assessing your service, make sure that the audit of psychological care is on the agenda. The sorts of questions that an audit group can ask about psychological care have been posed by Nichols (1989):

1. Are the staff involved properly trained in the relevant psychological techniques?
2. Is there an explicit scheme of psychological care with planned investigations?
3. Is there a planned allocation of psychological duties to staff?
4. Are clients allocated to staff for psychological care work in a systematic way?
5. Are there prepared materials?
6. Are records kept of the clients' psychological state and the nature of any interventions?
7. Is there provision for crisis intervention?
8. Is there a guarantee of psychological care for all the clients using the unit's service?

9. Is there a support and mutual supervision scheme for the staff running the scheme?

If you can answer 'yes' to all or even the majority of these questions, you are doing well. If you cannot do so, then areas where your service is lacking can become topics for local audit. Audit, of course, should be multidisciplinary and audit programmes should be SMART (see previous chapter).

Listen to the views of patients and carers

Do you know what your patients think about your service? Do you seek their views in a representative manner, or do you do so haphazardly, if at all? In the United Kingdom, recent legislation, consultation papers and the Patient's Charter have made clear the government's intention of making health services responsive to the views of patients and of involving them in their evaluation. This can be done in a number of ways: through formal management arrangements such as patient councils and representation on management groups, or through seeking patients' views individually or collectively on current services and future developments. When the views of patients are canvassed in a structured way, the results are remarkably consistent. For example, a survey in England by Hares et al. (1992) produced results that were very similar to the results of a survey performed in Sweden (Wikblad, 1991). There were considerable areas of overlap between the two. I have combined the results from them both into the following summary. The main requests from patients were for the following.

Continuity. Patients want to see the same staff on each visit because this allows a real relationship to develop.

Accessibility. Patients value having access to helpers at times when it is needed, rather than it being limited to fixed appointment times. Patients also value short waiting times and services that are available within easy travelling distance.

Consideration. This means being treated as an individual rather than as the originator of specimens and samples for laboratory reports. Patients want to be given choices and information that is relevant to their lifestyle and social circumstances.

Support. Patients ask for the opportunity to discuss fears and insecurities, including psychological and social factors. Carers and relatives also need support. Services such as home visits by nurse specialists are particularly valued.

Responsibility. Patients want staff to show trust in their ability to manage their own diabetes. They want to be given the necessary information that will allow them to take the responsibility for their own care.

Good technical skills. Patients need to know that the staff are competent professionals. They want all members of the team to be consistent with each other in the information that they give and the management practices that they recommend.

Education. Patients want staff to give patients the knowledge and the skills to manage their own disease. They want to be kept up to date with latest advances, and for their relatives to be kept informed as well.

Seeking the views of patients is particularly important. This is because, although their opinions sometimes match the views of professionals, sometimes they do not. In the paper by Hares, for example, the views of diabetes team members were also sought. Helpers underestimated the importance that patients placed upon information about diabetes and the treatment options that might be available to them. There were also differences between the views of patients with Type 1 diabetes and those with the Type 2 disorder. It is also important to remember that patients' views and priorities are not static. They are related to their developing experiences as they come to terms with and live with their disease. This means that seeking comments should be a regular feature of the service.

It is not difficult to carry out a survey of your patients' views. You can use questionnaires or structured interviews. If you have not done this before, it will help if you seek the advice of someone who is aware of the potential pitfalls. There will be people in your local department of clinical psychology who have the necessary skills and experience and who should be able to give you advice and support. Your local audit co-ordinator or quality manager might be able to help as well. If you do survey a sample of patients, do not forget that whatever changes you make, you will still need to take account of the individual needs of individual patients. A blanket response to provide, for example, more information for everyone is unlikely to be appropriate.

Develop Links with Specialist Resources

The type of psychological care that I have been discussing in this book is applicable to all patients by all helpers. Sometimes, however, you will come across a patient who has significant psychological problems with which you and the diabetes care team as a whole feel you cannot cope. This raises the question of links with specialist counselling or mental health services and the best way of co-ordinating care for such patients. One such case was Ms Green. I shall outline her story and then try to draw some conclusions about how to help patients when our personal skills or service resources are insufficient.

Ms Green's diabetes is what is sometimes described as brittle. That is, her blood glucose control is highly unstable, although there are no apparent physical reasons for it. Two thick volumes of medical case notes and a supplementary folder full of biochemistry reports indicate that the search for medical causes has been vigorous. She has had many admissions to hospital to try and regulate her control, but while her blood glucose rapidly stabilizes when she is on the ward, it becomes chaotic once she is discharged.

When she is admitted, her behaviour arouses strong passions among the staff. The suspicion that she uses her diabetes to achieve certain emotional ends cuts across the expectations we have for how patients should behave when they are ill. Staff feel used, and some want to reject her for abusing the facilities: 'beds are for the genuinely ill', is the feeling.

Like many patients whose control is brittle, Ms Green is in her early 20s, overweight and is on a surprisingly large amount of insulin. Like many such patients, there are family and emotional problems in her personal life.

Ms Green is an only child. Her father, an ex-army officer, is a difficult and demanding man, very cold and distant. Her mother is completely dominated by him. Family relationships are stormy. Recently, she has moved around the country changing jobs, never settling in one place long enough to develop roots or lasting friendships.

She was seen in casualty one weekend, having taken an overdose of her mother's sleeping tablets during a visit home. Staff were reluctant to send her home.

What is the best way to help Ms Green? Should she be cared for primarily by the mental health team, with support from the diabetes team? Or should it be the other way round; the mental health team providing support and advice for the diabetes team? On this occasion it was decided that she would be admitted to the psychiatric unit for assessment rather than to the medical ward:

While on the ward she was constantly asking staff to trust her to keep her insulin and syringes by herself and to regulate her own insulin injections. She insisted that hospital food was inappropriate and had lengthy sessions with the dietitian. The medical registrar was a regular visitor to the ward, answering her and the staff's queries concerning her management. The medical team felt there may be a medical cause for her instability. For their part, the psychiatric team were convinced the problems were largely psychological and behavioural. Despite all this, close supervision of her injections and regular self-monitoring of blood glucose resulted in excellent blood glucose control. On visits home, or following return from weekend leave, her blood glucose levels were noted to be wildly erratic.

Family counselling between the patient and her parents was attempted, but after two sessions she discharged herself and appears to have resumed her nomadic career.

The case of Ms Green illustrates a number of important points.

All helpers have a natural tendency to explain problems in terms of their own training. Physicians think first of medical explanations. As Tattersall (1985) pointed out, they have such an understandable fear of missing organic disease, that the possibility of a psychological explanation for patients' metabolic instability might not be readily accepted. Even if we do accept that this happens, we might then have a fixed view of the sort of patient who will behave in this way, and this will probably exclude those who are considered to be 'normal and nice'. Ms Green was socially skilled, well spoken and from a 'good family'; not at all the kind of patient one might expect to behave in such a way.

Where physical care and psychological care are carried out by two different teams, troubles are very difficult to avoid. At the time it seemed sensible to concentrate upon trying to manage the psychological problems using staff who were highly skilled in psychological care. In retrospect this led to confusion over roles and responsibilities. Had Ms Green stayed in contact with the psychiatric unit after her eventual discharge she would probably have been followed up by the psychiatric and the medical departments separately, giving further cause for confusion. It is better, wherever possible, that when additional counselling or psychotherapeutic help is required, expertise is devoted to the support of first-line diabetes care staff.

How could the problems of Ms Green have been managed differently? One way of achieving this is to have a counsellor or experienced mental health professional attached to the diabetes team. Lindsay (1985), a child psychiatrist, has described such an arrangement. She pointed out that a counsellor may not only help the members of the team understand the patients' reactions to them, but also the team members' reactions to the patients. At times helpers as well as patients may feel at the end of their tether. By being able to talk about their own feelings and conflicts, members of the team may be able to cope better themselves and with distress in their patients. She emphasizes the value of having time to discuss and therefore clarify the feelings of and about patients and families:

The team members bring to such discussions their knowledge and ideas about the family and in doing so often become more aware of what the problems really are and what they can do. The [counsellor] brings to the discussion knowledge of how children may react to difficult situations at different stages in their emotional development, how parents respond to their children and how families function. The appropriateness and practicality of plans can then be discussed and their implications to the family assessed. The understanding thus gained from discussions about the family may be used for others.

The paper by Lindsay contains a number of helpful examples of how emotional difficulties often lie behind difficulties in the control of diabetes and the importance of being able to identify and address them.

Even with the benefit of hindsight, it is difficult to say whether the availability of a counsellor within the team would have made a significant difference to the eventual outcome with Ms Green. At the very least a system for supporting the diabetes team would have been in place. Staff members would have felt stronger and better able to understand a patient showing such difficult behaviour. To minimize the chances of such disruptions occurring in your service, you need clear policies on what to do when you feel out of your psychological depth and clear channels of communication both within your team and with more specialist services. Does your diabetes service have a mechanism for formal interprofessional communication and information exchange?

The example I have just been discussing is a little out of the ordinary because patients who display brittle diabetes are unusual. More commonly you will see adolescents and young adults with eating disorders, and patients of all ages who are anxious or depressed. It is with patients such as all of these, however, that you are most likely to feel that you are working at the outer limits of your confidence and competence. The same principles apply: good communication, good support and access to a specialist opinion if necessary.

Developing Your Skills

If, as I hope, the previous chapters have whetted your interest in whole-person care, you will now be wondering how to develop your own skills further. There are a number of possibilities.

Read more

One way to start is to read more detailed texts. In this book I have taken a very practical approach and not gone too deeply into theoretical aspects of counselling. Once you start to broaden your reading, however, you will soon discover that there are a great many schools and models from which to choose. At some point you will have to decide which approach feels most comfortable for you. Some people say with pride that they are eclectic, taking whatever is valuable or useful to them from the various approaches but without becoming an apostle of any one particular theory. To such people an open mind is a receptive mind. Others heap scorn on this; to them an open mind signifies an empty head, and eclecticism is simply an excuse for an unwillingness or an inability to think the issues through. You will have to decide for yourself which school of thought you adopt.

First, some general books that might be helpful. I mentioned Egan in Chapter One. His book, *The Skilled Helper*, is a classic text and would form a useful starting point for further reading. Nichols (1993) has written a very practical book about developing psychological care in general hospital settings. His examples are mostly concerned with work in a renal unit. Davis and Fallowfield (1991) have edited a comprehensive book about counselling and communication in health care. General chapters on counselling theory and the importance of counselling and communication are supplemented by chapters dealing with specific illnesses, disorders and age groups. There is also a chapter on evaluating the effects of counselling and improved communication.

Concerning counselling and communication skills in more detail, Nelson-Jones (1993) has written a deservedly popular book, now in a third and much revised form. The book by Hargie et al. (1987) covers the range of interpersonal and communication skills that are required by helpers. It places sound practical advice in the context of psychological theory and research findings. Books by Mearns and Thorne (1988) on person-centred counselling; Dryden and Yankura (1993) on rational-emotive counselling; and Dryden and Feltham (1992) on brief counselling give useful practical introductions to some specific schools of counselling. Each contains a bibliography.

For a first-hand account of living with diabetes, *Metal Jam* (McLean, 1985) should not be missed. It is an instructive and readable account of the author's struggle with diabetes. She is a very articulate writer and must surely speak for many who share her experiences if not her command over words.

I have already mentioned the book by Maclean and Oram (1988) in relation to the exercises it contains for helping patients understand what diabetes means to them personally. It is full of quotations from patients about living with the disease. Kelleher (1988) also uses material derived from interviews with patients and their families to explore their experiences of living with diabetes.

For those who need to know more about the disease and its management, there are many textbooks available. *Diabetes Clinical Management* by Tattersall and Gale (1990) combines erudition with entertainment in equal measure, and is full of sound practical advice. *Psychology and Diabetes* (Shillitoe, 1988) remains the only comprehensive text covering psychological aspects. The best journals to scan are *Diabetic Medicine, Diabetes Care* and *Practical Diabetes*. *Diabetic Medicine* is published in England by Wiley and Sons, Ltd. *Diabetes Care* is published in the United States of America by the American Diabetes Association. Both journals publish reviews and articles concerning clinical research and practice. For readers whose primary need is for practical information and product news, *Practical Diabetes* should be read. It is published by PMH Medical Publications Ltd. Most readers should have access to these journals at their local postgraduate medical centre. Some readers may qualify for a free personal subscription to *Practical Diabetes*. Enquiries should be made to the publishers; their address is given at the end of the book.

Practise your skills

Counselling and communication skills are, as the words indicate, skills. That means that a key aspect of their acquisition lies in actually doing them. You can develop your understanding of the theoretical side of counselling, or of the psychology of interpersonal behaviour by reading about them, but there comes a point where there is no substitute for practical experience. This can be gained in a number of different ways, each of which has certain advantages and limits. They include observing others so that you learn from them; observing yourself so you learn to identify your strengths and learn from your mistakes; or being observed by others and learning from the subsequent feedback.

Observing others. Students often sit in with supervisors or more experienced colleagues and try to assimilate their skills while filtering out their bad habits. It is not always easy to tell the two apart, especially if you are fairly new to the field and have no one with whom to compare your model. Therefore, it is important that you choose appropriately skilled helpers as your model. One possibility is to listen to audio tapes or to watch videos of skilled practitioners in action. Tapes, and the written transcripts of sessions, are available from a number of sources. The British Association for Counselling has a catalogue of teaching materials that are available for hire (see the Appendix). Alternatively you could contact your local college of health or your own professional body.

Observing yourself. You can ask your patients for their permission to tape-record a session or two. It is best to be open about why you want to do this. When you make it clear that it is part of your personal development, most patients will be keen to help. They may even offer helpful comments and enquire about your progress next time you meet. Play your recordings back to yourself and ask yourself a series of questions as you do so. First, focus on the patient: 'What is the patient really saying?'; 'What emotions can I identify?'; 'What is the underlying message?' Next, focus on yourself; 'How do I sound'; 'Was I really listening?' 'Was I being empathic?' You can also try to identify ways in which your responses could have been improved. This method has the advantage of being flexible, but because you are doing it by yourself, progress is slow and without feedback. You can do the same with transcripts or tapes of acknowledged experts: cover up the response or stop the tape and devise your own reply; then compare it with the original. If you do tape a session, as you play it back count the number of times the telephone rings or someone tries the door. You may be surprised at the number of interruptions or the level of background noise.

Being observed. There may be a counselling skills self-help or support group nearby. Such settings provide a safe environment where participants can role-play being a patient and being a helper. You can then discuss how you felt in your respective roles. It is surprising how much you learn when you role-play the part of a patient; notice in particular how the helper's behaviour makes you feel. Nearly everyone hates role-play, but they learn a lot from it.

Going on training courses. Courses and workshops that combine theoretical with practical tuition are invaluable. They vary considerably in scope, orientation and duration, from the one-day workshop, to the fully fledged training course that might extend over a year or more. Something that satisfies your needs should be available locally. The BAC, local university or college, and your professional organization are the obvious starting points in your search for something suitable. The pressure on training budgets nowadays is immense. The pace of technical advances means that for many staff post-qualification training consists largely if not exclusively of technical updates, with little time or money left for training in whole-person care. It is important, therefore, if you and your manager meet regularly for appraisal interviews, you make sure that training in counselling skills is part of your personal development plan.

It may be possible to arrange for something less formal. For example, I mentioned relaxation training in Chapter Six. There is more to relaxation than just listening to a tape, however, as knowing how to apply the skills in real-life situations requires guidance. If you wish to teach relaxation skills, you will find it very helpful to receive some tuition and guided practice yourself before attempting to teach patients. Your local clinical psychology department or college of health might be able to help with support and training.

Get local support

Professional counsellors make sure that they have support networks and that supervision is part of their routine work. This supervision will include discussion of the counsellors' emotional reactions to their patients, as well as more general case-management issues. Counsellors are people who have chosen to work with patients who are emotionally disturbed or vulnerable, and have considerable training to help them do so. Even so, they find that support is invaluable. You are probably not a professional counsellor in this sense, but if you make yourself available to hear people and their stories, you also make yourself available to hear things that you will find painful, disturbing and unsettling. Your need for support will be no less than it is for the professional counsellor. It is very helpful to have someone with whom you can share such feelings in a confidential, supportive manner.

Can you identify such a person at your place of work? If you work in primary care, your practice may be one of the growing number that employs a counsellor on a sessional basis, and it may be possible for you to negotiate support from the counsellor as part of their duties. If you work in a hospital setting or diabetes centre, is there someone from the clinical psychology department with whom you can forge a link? There may be a psychotherapist somewhere in the system and some psychiatrists devote time to what is called liaison psychiatry. This is the mental heath aspects of physical medicine, and although few patients with diabetes will have a psychiatric disorder, many psychiatrists offer whole-person care and may be approached for support.

Without such support you may find that in order to cope with difficult emotions you begin to become hardened and start to distance yourself from the personal side of patient care. This is where we came in; the whole focus of your activities should be to ensure whole-person care.

Is It All Worthwhile?

Health workers are increasingly required to justify what they do, and to evaluate any changes they want to make to clinical practices. If you ask for funding to go on a training course to improve your counselling or communication skills, your manager will be very interested to hear in what ways the service will benefit as a result of your training. If you want to improve whole-person care, will this take up time and other resources that could be better used elsewhere? There are several ways in which you can approach these questions.

Research findings. The evidence that improving counselling and communication skills has positive benefits is considerable. It has been shown in a wide variety of clinical conditions and across a wide variety of health care settings. The benefits themselves are widespread. They include professional satisfaction with the job the helper does; patients' satisfaction with the services received; more accurate identification of problem areas (both physical and psychological) and more accurate performance of agreed care plans. The evidence has been summarized in detail by Davis and Fallowfield (1991). The interested reader will find that the weight of evidence is considerable. It is not as complete in the area of diabetes care as it is in respect of many other conditions, but there is no reason to believe that when the necessary studies have been done, the position will be found to be any different.

Political pressure. Next, patient choice and involvement are high on the political agenda. I have already written about the importance of listening to the views of patients. Listening is not enough. We have to take action upon what we hear. For us as helpers, to be responsive to the individual needs of different patients we have to engage them as active partners in our everyday clinical activities – as well as in the design of the service and its evaluation. To involve patients in a meaningful way and to give them choices requires us to be able to communicate with them effectively, and for us to bring to our work the attitude that values each as an individual along with their contributions.

Humanitarian reasons. Finally, you can go beyond the economic and political arguments and invoke the humanitarian. Here, you can do no better than adapt the case put forward by Nichols (1993). Imagine your partner or child has diabetes. There are two diabetes services from which to choose. One is technically good but is very traditional and puts little effort into keeping patients informed or caring for them at an emotional level. The other has staff who, as well as technical competence, have also been trained in the basic skills of psychological care. They will care for your partner or child emotionally in a professional way and offer counselling for any difficulties that arise. Which service would you choose, and why?

Summary

❑ There is no proven best model of service delivery. Irrespective of how they are organized, diabetes services should be planned with whole-person care in mind.

❑ Targets and standards should be set for whole-person care.

❑ A comprehensive service should measure psychological as well as physical and metabolic outcomes.

❑ It is necessary to have links with specialist mental health and counselling services. Specialist mental health workers can:

– support the first line diabetes team;

– contribute to the management of particularly difficult clinical problems.

❑ If you wish to develop your personal counselling and communication skills, you can:

– read books dealing with specific methods of counselling;

– observe skilled therapists, in real life, or with the help of video tapes, audio tapes or transcripts;

– tape your own sessions and analyse the recording;

– go on courses.

❑ Try to arrange local support and supervision.

❑ There are strong clinical, political and humanitarian arguments in support of whole-person care. It is, after all, the way you would like to be treated yourself.

References

Anderson, R. M. (1986) The personal meaning of having diabetes: Implications for patient behaviour and education. *Diabetes Care, 3*, 85–89.

Armstrong, D. (1991) The social context of technology in diabetes care: 'compliance' and 'control'. In C. Bradley, P. Home and M. J. Christie, (Eds) *The Technology of Diabetes Care*. Reading: Harwood Academic Publishers.

Bennett, P. (1993) *Counselling for Heart Disease*. Leicester: British Psychological Society.

Bradley, C. (Ed.) (1994, in press) *Handbook of Psychology and Diabetes: a guide to psychological measurement in diabetes research and practice*. Reading: Harwood Academic Publishers.

Bradley, C., and Gamsu, D. S. For the psychological well-being working party (1994 in press). Guidelines for encouraging psychosocial well-being: report of a working party of the World Health Organization Regional Office for Europe and International Diabetes Federation European Region St Vincent Declaration action programme for diabetes. *Diabetic Medicine*.

Bradley, C., Gamsu, D. S., Moses, J. L., et al. (1987) The use of diabetes-specific perceived control and health belief measures to predict treatment choice and efficacy in a feasibility study using continuous subcutaneous insulin infusion. *Psychology and Health, 1*, 133–146.

Brewin, T. B. (1991) Three ways of giving bad news. *The Lancet, 337*, 1207–1209.

Broome, A. K. (Ed.) (1989) *Health Psychology: Processes and Applications*. London: Chapman and Hall.

Buckman, R. (1992) *How to Break Bad News*. London: Papermac.

Davis, H. (1993) *Counselling Parents of Children with Chronic Illness or Disability*. Leicester: British Psychological Society.

Davis, H. and Fallowfield, L. (1991) *Counselling and Communication in Health Care*. Chichester: Wiley.

Diabetes Control And Complications Trial Research Group (1993) The effect of intensive treatment of diabetes on the development and progression of long-term complications in insulin-dependent diabetes mellitus. *New England Journal of Medicine, 329*, 977–986.

Dryden, W. and Feltham, D. (1992) *Brief Counselling*. Buckingham: Open University Press.

Dryden, W. and Yankura, J. (1993) *Counselling Individuals: A Rational-Emotive Handbook*, 2nd ed. London: Whurr Publishers.

Egan, G. (1986) *The Skilled Helper*, 3rd ed. Pacific Grove: Brooks/Cole.

Egger, M., Smith, G. D. and Teuscher, A. (1992) Human insulin and unawareness of hypoglycaemia: need for a large randomised trial. *British Medical Journal, 305*, 351–355.

Eiser, C. (1985) *The Psychology of Childhood Illness*. New York: Springer.

Gibson, C. H. (1991) A concept analysis of empowerment. *Journal of Advanced Nursing, 16*, 354–361.

Hares, T., Spencer, J., Gallagher, M., Bradshaw, C. and Webb, I. (1992) Diabetes care: who are the experts? *Quality in Health Care*, *1*, 219–224.

Hargie, O., Saunders, C. and Dickson, D. (1987) *Social Skills in Interpersonal Communication*, 2nd ed. London: Croom Helm.

Hess, G. E., Davis, W. G. and Van Harrison, R. (1986) A diabetes psychosocial profile. *Diabetes Education*, *12*, 135–140.

Hopson, B. (1982) Counselling and Helping. In J. Hall (Ed.) *Psychology for Nurses and Health Visitors*. London: British Psychological Society and Macmillan Publishers Ltd.

Kelleher, D. (1988) *Diabetes*. The Experience of Illness Series. London: Routledge and Kegan Paul.

Ley, P. (1988) *Communicating with Patients*. London: Chapman and Hall.

Lindsay, M. (1985) Emotional management. In J. D., and A-L. Kinmonth (Eds) *Care of the Child with Diabetes*. Edinburgh: Churchill Livingstone.

Maguire, P. and Faulkener, A. (1988a) How to do it: communicate with cancer patients: 1 Handling bad news and difficult questions. *British Medical Journal*, *297*, 907–909.

Maguire, P. and Faulkener, A. (1988b) How to do it: communicate with cancer patients: 2 Handling uncertainty, collusion and denial. *British Medical Journal*, *297*, 972–974.

MacLean, H. and Oram, B. (1988) *Living with Diabetes: Personal Stories and Strategies for Coping*. Toronto: University of Toronto Press.

McLean, T. (1985) *Metal Jam: The Story of a Diabetic*. London: Hodder and Stoughton.

Mearns, D. and Thorne, B. (1988) *Person-Centred Counselling in Action*. London: Sage.

Miller, J. F. (1983) Enhancing self-esteem. In J. F. Miller. (Ed.) *Coping with Chronic Disease*. Philadelphia: F. A. Davis.

Nelson-Jones, R. (1983) *Practical Counselling Skills*. London: Holt, Rinehart and Winston.

Nelson-Jones, R. (1993) *Practical Counselling and Helping Skills*, 3rd ed. London: Cassell.

Nichols, K. A. (1989) Psychological care, counselling and diabetes, Part 1: principles and practice. *Diabetes Care*, *6*, 359–360.

Nichols, K. A. (1993) *Psychological Care In Physical Illness*, 2nd ed. London: Chapman and Hall.

Nichols, K. A. and Jenkinson, J. (1991) *Leading a Support Group*. London: Chapman and Hall.

North Tyneside Diabetes Team (1992) The diabetes annual review as an educational tool: assessment and learning integrated with care, screening and audit. *Diabetes Care*, *9*, 389–394.

Parrott, A. (1990) Diabetes management: viewpoint of the patient. *Practical Diabetes*, *7*, 114–118.

Porritt, L. (1990) *Interaction Strategies*, 2nd ed. Edinburgh: Churchill-Livingstone.

Schafer, L. C., McCaul, K. D. and Glasgow, R. E. (1986) Supportive and non-supportive family behaviours: relationships to adherence and metabolic control in persons with Type 1 diabetes. *Diabetes Care, 9,* 179–185.

Schwartz, L. S. (1988) My sweetness problem. *Diabetic Medicine, 5,* 396–398.

Shillitoe, R. W. (1988) *Psychology and Diabetes: Psychological Factors in Management and Control.* London: Chapman and Hall.

Shillitoe, R. W. (1991) Counselling in health care: diabetes mellitus. In H. Davis and L. Fallowfield (Eds) *Counselling and Communication in Health Care.* Chichester: Wiley.

Tattersall, R. B. (1985) Brittle diabetes. *British Medical Journal, 291,* 555–557.

Tattersall, R. B. and Gale, E. A. M. (Eds) (1990) *Diabetes Clinical Management.* Edinburgh, Churchill Livingstone.

Ternulf Nyhlin, K. (1990) Diabetic patients facing long-term complications: coping with uncertainty. *Journal of Advanced Nursing, 15,* 1021–1029.

Thomas, D. (1984) A dad's view of diabetes. *Practical Diabetes, 1,* 13–15.

Thompson, J. (1984) Compliance. In R. Fitzpatrick et al. (Ed.) *The Experience of Illness.* London: Tavistock Publications.

Trower, P., Casey, A. and Dryden, W. (1988). *Cognitive Behavioural Counselling in Action.* London: Sage.

Ward, J. D. and MacKinnon, M. (1992) Diabetes care. *Quality in Health Care, 1,* 260–265.

Wikblad, K. F. (1991) Patient perspectives of diabetes care and education. *Journal of Advanced Nursing, 16,* 837–844.

Appendix

Useful addresses
American Diabetes Association
1660 Duke Street
Alexandria, Va 22314

British Association of Counselling
1 Regent Place
Rugby, Warwickshire CV21 2PJ

British Diabetic Association
10 Queen Anne Street
London W1M 0BD

Index

COMMUNICATION AND COUNSELLING

COUNSELLING FOR HEART DISEASE

Paul Bennett

'Should be mandatory reading for all those who treat cardiac patients'
Health Psychology Update

A heart attack is a physically devastating event involving an immediate threat to life. The psychological and social impact can have an adverse effect on the individual, the family and on the disease itself.

This book provides a practical framework both for the acute medical setting and, in the longer term, in the community. There are sections on:

- how to convey important information to patients who are distressed or in shock;
- stress management training and goal-setting during rehabilitation;
- risk factor intervention.

Paul Bennett is a Principal Clinical Psychologist with Gwent Psychological Services and a lecturer in health psychology.

1993, 144 pp
1 85433 096 pb, 1 85433 092 6 hb

COUNSELLING PARENTS OF CHILDREN WITH CHRONIC ILLNESS OR DISABILITY

Hilton Davis

'I would advise all those working with children to obtain a copy.'
Community Outlook

Diagnosis of a chronic childhood disease or disability is a major crisis, bringing with it irreversible change for the whole family.

Child health care tends to neglect the psychosocial needs of the family as a whole. This book aims to help medical staff and carers relate to parents in ways that facilitate their adaptation to their child's illness. The essence of this help is communication.

Detailed attention is given to establishing a partnership with parents, setting goals and developing problem-solving strategies.

Hilton Davis is Head of Child & Adolescent Psychology, and Clinical Director of Child Mental Health at Lewisham & Guy's Mental Health Trust.

1993, 144 pp
1 85433 091 8 pb, 1 85433 090 X hb

IN HEALTH CARE SERIES

COUNSELLING IN OBSTETRICS AND GYNAECOLOGY

Myra Hunter

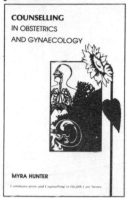

COUNSELLING
IN OBSTETRICS
AND GYNAECOLOGY

MYRA HUNTER
Communication and Counselling in Health Care Series

'This is a very well written book ... the psychology is sound and it will be a useful reference for many health professionals and volunteers working with women of any age.'
Health Psychology Update

Almost every woman has her tale to tell: embarrassment, misunderstandings and discomfort are common reactions to obstetric and gynaecological experiences.

This book describes women's concerns over a broad range of problems and interventions. Most women want to be fully informed and to be included in treatment decisions.

Detailed attention is given to issues such as preparing women for surgery, breaking bad news and providing support before, during and after childbirth.

Myra Hunter is a Chartered Clinical Psychologist working in obstetrics and gynaecology at University College Hospital, and Research Fellow/Senior Lecturer at Guy's Hospital Medical School.

January 1994, 144 pp
1 85433 119 1 pb, 1 85433 118 3 hb

Supportive communication is central to all aspects of clinical practice and health care: the first meeting; exploratory tests and diagnosis; treatment and nursing. Establishing a positive working partnership with patients can greatly influence prognosis and recovery.

This series provides guidelines which show, using case material, how to improve counselling and communication skills to meet patients' needs for more sensitivity and responsiveness. The books are aimed at all health care workers - specialist and general, professional and voluntary. They will also be read by many patients and their families. Inspection copies are available to course tutors.

Titles in preparation:

COUNSELLING CHILDREN WITH CHRONIC MEDICAL CONDITIONS
Melinda Edwards & Hilton Davis

COUNSELLING PEOPLE WITH VISIBLE DISFIGUREMENT
Eileen Bradbury

COUNSELLING IN TERMINAL CARE & BEREAVEMENT
Colin Murray Parkes, Marilyn Relf & Ann Couldrick